Recipe for
Great
Teaching

T0071991

Recipe for
Great
Teaching

11
Essential
Ingredients

Anita Moultrie Turner
Foreword by Andrea Maxie

Skyhorse Publishing

Copyright © 2007 by Corwin Press
First Skyhorse Publishing edition 2015

All rights reserved. No part of this book may be reproduced in any manner without the express written consent of the publisher, except in the case of brief excerpts in critical reviews or articles. All inquiries should be addressed to Skyhorse Publishing, 307 West 36th Street, 11th Floor, New York, NY 10018.

Skyhorse Publishing books may be purchased in bulk at special discounts for sales promotion, corporate gifts, fund-raising, or educational purposes. Special editions can also be created to specifications. For details, contact the Special Sales Department, Skyhorse Publishing, 307 West 36th Street, 11th Floor, New York, NY 10018 or info@skyhorsepublishing.com.

Skyhorse® and Skyhorse Publishing® are registered trademarks of Skyhorse Publishing, Inc.®, a Delaware corporation.

Visit our website at www.skyhorsepublishing.com.

10 9 8 7 6 5 4 3 2 1

Library of Congress Cataloging-in-Publication Data is available on file.

Print ISBN: 978-1-63220-567-4
Ebook ISBN: 978-1-63220-983-2

Printed in the United States of America

Contents

Foreword

Many years ago, I had the honor of working with a team of talented teachers to build an innovative global studies curriculum. Our work together allowed us to enter each other's workplaces—the public school and the university—as we struggled with new ideas and concepts and their meaning for teaching, learning, and schooling. Though our focus was curriculum, we learned that this could never be separate from our beliefs about good teaching and powerful learning. Indeed, we saw good teaching as the centerpiece of student learning. For all of us, good teaching mattered. And one of us has captured that in *Recipe for Great Teaching: 11 Essential Ingredients*.

Anita Moultrie Turner probes the science and art of pedagogy as she shares her professional wisdom, personal stories of teaching, passion for excellence, and sound knowledge base about teacher effectiveness. We are privileged to enter the thinking of a great teacher, to see how she skillfully and artfully weaves together her relationship with students, knowledge of pedagogy, and professional dispositions. Whether beginning teacher or seasoned veteran, all of us can learn from the practice of teaching illustrated throughout this book.

Early on, the book grounds us in appropriate dispositions about students and the work of teaching. From there, we are taken through the complexities of teaching, including knowledge of students, strategies for building effective learning environments, techniques for successful curriculum planning, methods for engaging all students in learning, and ways of working with colleagues and the community. We are treated to the special tips that a gifted professional can offer. We are dazzled by the enthusiasm that an exemplary teacher exudes. Ultimately, we are challenged to reflect on our own work.

Recipe for Great Teaching: 11 Essential Ingredients is a learning tool that honors the dignity of teaching and the teaching profession.

Andrea Maxie, PhD
Professor of Education
California State University, Los Angeles

Preface

*G*reat is defined as powerful, excellent, skilled, and influential. When I use this word throughout the text, I am absolutely convinced that a great teacher has the capacity to execute every trait as defined to make a lifelong impact on the lives of his or her students.

Teaching is not an easy profession. Being a great teacher involves many factors, which, when combined correctly, result in a highly effective classroom and productive students. Each of the "ingredients" listed in this book is essential to achieving the goal of being a great teacher, but the "recipe" for excellent teaching requires the right mixture of all the ingredients.

Students come to the classroom with a variety of skills, talents, challenges, and experiences. Teachers come to the classroom only after navigating their way through an extraordinary number of school, district, and state policies; state-adopted textbooks; mandated reading and math programs; inclusion requirements; high-stakes standardized tests; standards-based instructional programs; and administrative pressures. Teaching is obviously not a "piece of cake."

The true test of great classroom learning has to start with the teacher as "chef": setting out the ingredients on the table, measuring the value of each, and determining daily how best to "serve it up" to meet the unique and individual academic, social, emotional, and moral needs of each student.

This effort requires ongoing reflection by the teacher to determine how to season each dish to suit each student's taste. A great teacher knows that the classroom is not a "cattle call" where everyone gets the same information in the same way at the same time. What works for one child may not work for the next. Instead, a pinch of this and a dash of that will allow students to experience a different flavor for each lesson, appropriate to the student's individual "palate" of intelligences, strengths, and learning modalities.

This book is not a cookbook or encyclopedia that answers every question for every teacher. But it is an opportunity for you to visit the workplace and go inside the heart and mind of a seasoned teacher who heard a "call to greatness" in the classroom and successfully mastered the art of creating a learning environment in which students experienced a nourishing and well-balanced academic feast.

Acknowledgments

I am grateful for being called into this profession. I appreciate the love and support of my children Mark, Aerick, Arianna, and Amani.

I would like to thank the countless colleagues, mentors, and fellow educators who influenced my development as a great teacher.

Thanks to the many students who made a difference in my life. Hopefully, in some small way, I made a difference in their lives as well!

Skyhorse Publishing gratefully thanks the following reviews for their contributions to this book:

Patricia Bowman, Principal
C. Morley Sellery School, Gardena, CA

Scott Braxton, Director of Senior High Students
Local District 7, Los Angeles Unified School District,
Los Angeles, CA

Patricia F. Clark, First-Grade Teacher
Gotham Avenue School, Elmont, NY

John Pieper, Fifth-Grade Teacher
Webster Stanley Elementary School, Oshkosh, WI

Kathleen Prisbell, National Board Certified Teacher,
Teacher of English/Curriculum Council Chair
Russell O. Brackman Middle School, Barnegat, NJ

Tammy Shifflett, Science Teacher
C. A. Roberts Elementary, Dallas, GA

About the Author

 **Anita Moultrie Turner** has been a teacher, teacher-trainer, mentor teacher, department chair, and instructional advisor for both schools and school districts in Los Angeles, California. At Washington Preparatory High School, the student body voted her Most Outstanding Teacher and awarded her a golden apple trophy for three consecutive years. At Crenshaw High School, the students voted her Outstanding Teacher of the Year in three of their eight categories.

Anita is also a lecturer, guest speaker, and presenter at career days, retreats, conventions, workshops, conferences, and other special events. She is active in radio and television broadcasting and was featured on Channel 11 news as one of the top 10 educators in Los Angeles. She received an Emmy nomination for co-producing a six-part instructional video series titled *Teachers and Their Coaches*. Anita has written several books, and her teaching style was presented in the novel *And Still We Rise* by Miles Corwin. Anita also served as the founding principal of Accelerated Charter High School in Los Angeles. Anita Moultrie Turner has been the literacy director for the Urban Education Partnership, in which she supervised literacy coaches in five middle schools. Currently, she is the instructional specialist at Charles R. Drew Middle School in Los Angeles Unified School District and an adjunct professor in the Charter College of Education at California State University at Los Angeles.

Visit Anita's Web site at www.harvest4success.com.

Passion and Compassion

The Power of a Great Teacher

The primary ingredient for the making of a great teacher is love. This simple word, however, creates a multifaceted influence on your effectiveness and success in the classroom.

LOVE YOURSELF: LEAVING A POWERFUL IMPACT ON YOUNG MINDS

You have to love yourself before you can effectively reach out and educate young and impressionable minds. It is important that you are secure in your own emotions, self-esteem, and qualifications.

It is important that you see yourself as a dynamic influence, as a nurturer in the nest of your own classroom filled with eager, hungry, young minds and spirits. The teacher who embraces the challenge of igniting in children a love for subject content, a love for learning, and a love for themselves at the same time can have a tremendously powerful impact. A teacher who loves himself or herself is a teacher who can love others. These teachers are the candles that light other candles, but retain the same amount of light of their own.

Teaching can be tiring, frustrating, and complicated at times. Whether new or veteran, I strongly recommend that teachers maintain a hobby, take a vacation, take a long soothing bubble bath, or romp in the park with their own children. It is important that teachers keep their lives balanced between the personal and the professional. I often challenge teachers to gaze in the mirror and assess who they are as people and all the reasons why they feel it critical to take on the role of a teacher. Ultimately, inspiration and education are the products of teachers giving themselves as a gift to students. A great teacher possesses self-love, which frees him or her to extend love to others.

YOU ARE A ROLE MODEL

As educators, you are truly role models for your students. Even in this highly technological world, young people still look for people they can admire, respect, and emulate.

Each teacher must consider that even if a particular standard for appropriate dress may not be required in your contract, it is important that you are sensitive to the culture of your school and what your colleagues have collectively established as appropriate dress for your workplace. There are schools that have teachers wear a uniform. This may include certain slacks, jackets, or shirts or blouses displaying the school's logo, mascot, or mission statement. There are other schools in which teachers wear suits, dresses, skirts, or slacks. Still other schools may allow teachers to dress at their own discretion, whether casual or dressy. It truly depends on the dynamics and culture of each particular school. Given these considerations, it is important to remember our conscientious efforts to dress appropriately will maintain the integrity of our profession.

As role models, teachers should also be very careful to avoid the use of profanity, gossip, or criticism of others in front of students. This type of unprofessional behavior will totally influence the students' perception of you, not the person being discussed within their earshot.

In addition, students can read us like a book (pun intended). They know if we are having a good day or a bad day. As much as is humanly possible, then, you should avoid giving overt indicators in your instructional day that you are dealing with personal problems. You must make a conscientious effort not to allow unpleasant personal circumstances to impact your potential for effectively instructing your students.

It is important to avoid discussing at length your own problems with the students. I have heard students say, "I'm so tired of hearing about Mrs. ____'s defiant son. It isn't that we don't care. It's just that we get tired of hearing about it all the time!" It is all right, however, for students to clearly understand that teachers are people too. Teachers have families, feelings, and challenges in their own lives, and these may affect their mood, temperament, or delivery of instruction. It is better for teachers to be completely honest with students and not take their personal frustrations out on them. As relationships are strengthened overall, there should develop a sensitivity and concern for each member of the classroom, including the teacher.

As a great teacher, you must say to yourself, "No matter what I am going through, the students deserve my best. If I give them my best, then I can require the best from them." When students admire their teachers, respect closely follows.

LOVE YOUR STUDENTS: ENGAGING THE POTENTIAL IN EACH STUDENT

You have to love your students. Yes, I know, I know . . . sometimes they can be unbearable. But a great teacher can love the child without necessarily loving some of the unproductive behavior he or she may exhibit in the classroom. As teachers, we must see the good in every student. No child is all bad;

that's just not how we were created. It has been my experience that students will accept the challenge toward excellence when they know that their teacher genuinely loves and respects them and that he or she is concerned about their development as a complete and mature human being.

Some of the worst students in your classroom right now are probably some of the brightest. Great teachers look not just at what students do, but also at what they don't do. They listen to what the students say, but also to what they don't say. Behavior is a form of communication. In other words, it is important not to take everything about the children at face value. A student may not be able to articulate why he or she exhibits inappropriate behavior, but if you dig deeper into the problem and look beyond the outward behavior, I believe that you will uncover an intelligent, creative, and responsive child.

Great teachers realize that a child's abilities are not contingent solely on socioeconomic status, appearance, geographic location, or the presence of both parents in the home. Children are not necessarily assigned intelligence, creativity, wit, and curiosity on the basis of the neighborhood in which they live. Some of our most noteworthy leaders, of all nationalities, have come from modest beginnings. A great teacher, then, loves his or her students for what they can become, not necessarily for what they appear to be during this snapshot of time at a particular grade level.

LOVE THE PROFESSION OF TEACHING

Last, great teachers love the profession of teaching. Teachers have many responsibilities other than being the "giver of knowledge." You may often find yourself expected to fill the role of surrogate parent, tutor, nurse, counselor, security blanket, psychologist, social worker . . . and the list goes on. Some people have the misconception that our occupation must be easy because schoolchildren are dismissed in the late afternoon, we typically don't work weekends, and we are paid on most major holidays. Pshaw!

Teachers spend countless hours outside of the school day calling parents and guardians at home or work, preparing lessons, correcting papers, and keeping records of grades and attendance. Elementary teachers must respond to 20 to 30 different students, and most secondary teachers encounter more than 100 preteens and teenagers every day. Teachers often feel that they are not adequately compensated for these laborious duties and for wearing all their numerous "hats." It can be a thankless job.

Great educators, however, teach because they love being in this profession. They fully understand that the rewards are not always monetary. They relish the opportunity to observe the "lightbulb" of understanding turn on in a child's brain, to witness the emergence of self-esteem in a child whose confidence was once shattered, to see a disposition change from bitterness to happiness, and to see a negative attitude become a positive one and failing grades turn into honor roll grades. These rewards cannot be measured in silver or gold.

THE POWER OF ONE: ENCOURAGING ACADEMIC EXCELLENCE

Teachers must look at themselves as having the "power of one." Every teacher has the awesome responsibility to educate and influence the lives of young people. They have the power to compel, encourage, challenge, entreat, and motivate children to achieve excellence beyond their own expectations. Teachers can expand horizons, open opportunities, stretch imaginations, and tap intellectual capabilities in the educational womb of the classroom. This may ultimately influence students' decisions to become doctors, lawyers, educators, ministers, architects, entrepreneurs, politicians, presidents, and CEOs. Who knows—in your classroom, right now, may be the child who grows up to discover a cure for AIDS or cancer, facilitate world peace, or eliminate worldwide hunger and poverty.

Step proudly into this honorable position. Accept your calling as a great educator, and watch how the power of your role as an educator can influence a change that is greater than what you could ever have hoped or imagined. Your passion for teaching and your compassion for students will have a far-reaching impact on your life as well as the lives of your students!

It is vital to really get to know your students—likes and dislikes, joys and challenges, talents and dispositions, goals and aspirations. In addition, it is essential to make contact with your students' families, become acquainted with the neighboring community, and determine the resources, both on and off the campus, that can assist you with meeting the needs of your students. Most schools have resources and professionals both on staff and in the community that will be instrumental in providing ongoing academic, mental, physical, and emotional supports.

True Story

I had a high school student who declared that she hated me and conducted herself in a manner that pricked my last nerve. I continued to love this tormented and tormenting human being. She tried everything she could to upset me: tardy to my class, disrupted lessons, used profanity, turned in homework late, if at all . . .

One day, I had enough of her antics. I took her by the hand as if she were a six-year-old child and walked her to the dean's office. I told her that I loved her very much and it brought me much despair and unhappiness to know that she refused to cooperate and learn in my class. After we talked, I returned to my classroom and prayerfully resolved that I had done everything in my power to show her how much I cared.

She later admitted that she was very unhappy because of personal problems. She thanked me for showing her uncon-ditional love. I was able to secure the much-needed assistance she needed to begin the healing process. We have continued to stay in contact with one another over the years. This same rebellious and defiant young lady is now a minister, preaching to and teaching others about the love of God.

Extra Seasoning

A Person's Perception Is His or Her Reality

Students have preconceived notions or perceptions of how a teacher should act, dress, and speak. Whether you are a novice teacher or a seasoned veteran, students will offer you their highest esteem if you present yourself in a professional manner. Your love for them will foster the practice of looking beyond outward appearances to touch the heart of each child. In fact, great teachers fully understand that they will affect not only the lives of individual children; they also touch the lives of the children's families and communities.

Savory Morsel

To find the good in the world, start with a mirror.

—Kamau

Reflection Menu

- What are your reasons for becoming a teacher (other than the money and benefits)?
- How do your impressions about yourself (background, culture, religion, biases) influence your perceptions and treatment of students?
- Why is love an absolutely essential ingredient for your effectiveness in the classroom?

If You Like This Ingredient, You'll Also Like . . .

Ingredient 3

Ingredient 10

Communication

An Essential Ingredient

THE EDUCATOR: "25 NOT 5"

It has been my observation that many teachers instruct 5 to 10 students in their class instead of 25 or 30! The other 20 or so sit idly with their brainwaves registering academic comatose ... not having heard much of anything discussed because class participation is rarely required of them.

A great teacher, however, teaches the entire class. While conducting discussion or disseminating information, ask for feedback from everyone in the classroom. A child who is reluctant about raising his or her hand can also experience a measure of success. For example, when the "raised hand" answers a question correctly, repeat the answer for everyone to hear, then ask an "unraised hand" to repeat, clarify, or expound on what was just stated.

These responses should also be rewarded with a friendly and warm compliment. Using this technique eventually creates an environment in which all 25 or 30 students become actively involved in class discussions. It is also one successful way to challenge students to become more attentive, responsible, and accountable for their own learning.

We want students to "buy into" their own learning ... take ownership ... become active participants! Therefore, it is absolutely essential that students are afforded frequent opportunities to respond orally, which reinforces comprehension, communication, and critical-thinking skills. We want the children to be literate in each content area by communicating verbally or in written form the information we are teaching them each day through the effective use of content vocabulary, information, pedagogy, and other resources. Students should be able to successfully apply their knowledge in similar or varying situations. They should also make connections with other subject areas as well as real-life experiences. This provides clear and measurable indicators of whether the students have truly learned the content subject matter.

Ultimately, the true test of exemplary instruction is not how well the teacher knows the content material, but rather how well students are able to articulate and execute a variety of concepts and skills. A great educator knows that there is a difference between teaching and learning!

No Favoritism: No Teacher's Pet

Favoritism should not exist in a great teacher's classroom. A great teacher should allow every student to feel special by equitably giving compliments, praise, encouragement, and assistance in the classroom.

It is also extremely effective to alternate the students' responsibilities as monitors, class leaders, runners, or helpers. This gives them a sense of belonging! Communicate to every child that his or her presence in your room is welcomed and makes a difference in the success of the day. Students are each unique and bring specific qualities, skills, and talents to the full group.

It must be clearly communicated to students every day that they are an integral part of a "community of learners." This applies to students of all ages! Remember also to give each child the same amount of time to respond to a question. Do not give the child you favor 20 seconds to answer and the unfavored child only 5 seconds! In addition, if the student does not respond correctly, then the teacher must diplomatically ask other students to assist the first child or ask the child to call on another person to provide him or her with assistance.

Warning: When a teacher frequently calls on a specific child or a few children, this communicates the wrong message to the masses!

NONVERBAL MESSAGES

Communication does not always involve sounds, phrases, or sentences. Teachers also send out nonverbal messages to their students. This may include gestures (head, arm, or hand movements), facial expressions, or other movements of the body. It could also include taking a deep and exaggerated breath, sighing, and rolling the eyes.

A teacher's attitude can be made even more evident by those nonverbal gestures! Unfortunately, students who feel that a teacher has a negative attitude will respond in like manner. In fact, I have seen children of all ages totally shut down and refuse to participate in class or achieve to their maximum academic potential because they felt that the teacher did not like them. They have decided in their young minds that if the teacher has an attitude, then they will have an attitude, too!

It has been my experience that a greater effort is generally made by students to maintain a positive attitude if the teacher consistently displays a positive attitude with them.

The moral of the story is . . . keep your verbal and non-verbal messages positive. A warm smile, direct eye contact, proximity, compliments, and encouragement are all powerful incentives for students to achieve great success in your classroom!

CALL HOME: OPEN COMMUNICATION WITH PARENTS

As great teachers, it is absolutely essential to keep a line of communication open between you and parents. Of course, with all the many responsibilities you have both personally and professionally, you probably do not call home until the child has done something wrong.

A great way to open the school year is to initially call home with a positive statement about each child or share compliments with parents during Open House. Any follow-up conversations, then, will likely diminish the possibility of parents becoming defensive, negative, or uncooperative.

It is also a good idea to initiate the telephone conversation by discussing ways in which the child is doing well or improving before discussing the disruptive behavior or poor academic performance. This puts the parents at ease and allows for more productive communication. As a sensitive and conscientious teacher, be very careful to choose your words wisely.

The following is a scenario to demonstrate appropriate and inappropriate ways to discuss the same information with a parent regarding his or her child's performance in your class:

Teacher 1: Your child is terrible in class and no one wants to sit next to him; therefore, I isolated him in the back of the room where he belongs!

Teacher 2: Your child has been doing very well in math and English, but I do have a concern that he is talking quite a bit during class time. This prevents him from completing his own work, and it causes a distraction for some of the other students as well.

Remember that even your worst student may be the apple of his or her parent's eye: "Oh, no," exclaims the astonished parent, "my baby couldn't have done that!" Encourage the parents to suggest some strategies to resolve the problem and possible ways that they can assist you at home. Entreat parents to partner with you to devise solutions and strategies for the improvements needed for their child. Remember that it is important to set up benchmarks in time or outcomes to monitor the progress of these agreements.

REFRAIN FROM MAKING ANY VALUE JUDGMENTS!

Great teachers avoid the inaccurate perception that disruptive children probably have parents who are callous or uninvolved with their children.

This is absolutely incorrect!

Most of the parents that I have encountered over the years were caring people who were greatly concerned about their child's behavior in school and very willing to render help in resolving any problem. Even if the parent is not necessarily cooperative, your professionalism can bring healing to the situation.

Therefore, handle all calls home diplomatically. You never want to offend the parent. It is always best to have the support of parents, because they play a vital role in the emotional, intellectual, psychological, and physical development of your students.

The old adage that parents are a child's first teacher must be seriously considered!

PARENT CONFERENCES

During Open House, Back to School Night, and parent conferences, it is essential that teachers are professional, diplomatic, and caring in their communication skills. There is absolutely nothing beneficial when teachers criticize a parent's handling of a child at home. It is not your place, as the teacher, to impute value judgments, biases, or predisposed notions and share them with the parents. Instead, a great teacher should use a strong, reflective conversational approach with parents, which includes actively listening, and paraphrasing and clarifying information rather than lecturing, demeaning, reprimanding, or scolding them.

True Story 1

Parent Conference night was fast approaching, and a faculty meeting was held by the administrative team at my school. The team reviewed the logistics and shared helpful suggestions for each teacher's appropriate and professional conduct in this type of setting.

The night of the parent conference, I was sitting in my class talking to a parent while seven or eight other parents waited patiently to see me. Suddenly, we all heard a loud raucous noise in a nearby classroom and rushed into the hallway to see if we might provide assistance. Security had been called because a teacher had verbally lashed out at a student and her parents. The father became angry and kicked over a chair. As this conversation reached its boiling point, the father gave her a "tongue lashing" that she wouldn't soon forget.

The next day, the same parents checked their daughter out of that teacher's classroom. The catalyst that caused this explosive situation was that the teacher hurled a series of demeaning and insulting accusations at the parents. It totally alienated the parents, and the outcome was much different than anyone expected, especially this teacher.

Instead of "going there," teachers must patiently share with parents strategies that everyone can implement together to encourage the child. If asked for suggestions to help at home, be honest and specific. The teacher should state the task to be learned or improved and how it can be accomplished. You may also share ways in which these goals will be reinforced each day in the classroom and how parents can assist at home.

Before ending the conversation, the teacher and parent should set up a time for contacting one another again to consider how well the plan is working at home and school. A great teacher's communication should be direct, sensitive, firm, and positive. Parents really respect and appreciate a teacher who shares clear and succinct suggestions that will benefit their child. If communicated in a positive, sensitive, and respectful manner, the parent will become a strong ally to assist you in meeting the goals established in your classroom.

LUNCHROOM CONVERSATIONS

As great teachers, be very careful of the conversations you have with your colleagues. I call these the "lunchroom conversations." Of course, this is not true in every teachers' cafeteria, but I have observed that the lunchroom can be a cesspool for teachers who complain about students and make some of the most unkind comments about them in the lunchroom, such as:

- How dumb kids are
- How they hate teaching "these kids"
- How the students' parents probably don't care about them
- How they are at the school to "save" these poor students

What you communicate in your own mind and with other colleagues will ultimately influence how you treat the students in your classroom each day.

THE STUDENTS: FACTORS INFLUENCING EFFECTIVE ORAL COMMUNICATION

Theme: People Are Judged on the Basis of How Well They Communicate

There are at least four important factors in students' oral communication and presentation skills that can be successfully integrated into the teacher's daily classroom activities.

Posture—Ask your students to sit up in their chairs. No slouching! No slumping! Good posture can lend itself to a student's attention to the lesson and the ability to listen critically and comprehend the information being discussed. In addition, create opportunities in class for students to perform presentations. Excellent posture should include a straight spine, with the chin up, arms relaxed at the sides, feet together, and shoulders set back. I call this a "power position"!

Voice Projection/Intonation—Encourage your students to speak up when communicating orally with others. They should not have a docile, quiet, meek voice, but rather one of strength, dignity, and confidence. I tell my students to speak as one with authority and power. They are not to have weak, wimpy voices . . . who will listen to them? A voice that commands another person's attention is more likely to speak words most remembered by its listeners.

The teacher should also consistently project a voice that will allow every student in the class to hear him or her. The student in the last row should be able to hear the lesson just as well as the student in the first row.

Eye Contact—Since public speaking is one of humankind's most common fears, people may compensate for their nervousness by looking down or frequently gazing at the ceiling (as if the speech were written up there!). Emphasize to your developing orators that establishing eye contact is an effective strategy for drawing the audience into their spoken words.

To assist my students with the development of good eye contact, I would say "good morning" or "good afternoon" to every student as I greeted him or her at the door or completed attendance each day. The students must establish eye contact with me and respond in like manner. This daily routine can reinforce their self-esteem and also build a greater rapport between you and your students! It is important to note that eye contact with students also improves their time on task and reduces disciplinary issues.

Complete Sentences—Students should be required to speak in complete sentences. This can include incorporating a part of the teacher's question into the student's response.

Example:

Question: What is your name?

Answer: My name is Alexis.

Question: Who was the African American man recognized for leading nonviolent civil rights demonstrations?

Answer: The African American man recognized for leading nonviolent civil rights demonstrations was Dr. Martin Luther King, Jr.

What purpose does this serve?

- Dissuades students from giving one-word responses
- Dissuades students from starting sentences with "because"
- Allows students time to process the information
- Hones the students' ability to listen and think critically
- Enhances writing skills. Students who speak in complete sentences are more likely to write in complete sentences as well
- Encourages the expansion of one's vocabulary, which includes effective use of "subject-specific language"— math, social studies, English, science, etc.
- Promotes standard-English proficiency
- Develops marketable verbal skills
- Builds confidence and self-esteem

STANDARD-ENGLISH ACQUISITION

Why Should Students Be Encouraged to Speak in Standard English?

Many second-language speakers have difficulty effectively articulating information in standard English. They come to the school setting speaking a different language, which may cause them some difficulties in their assignments, oral participation, and standardized or teacher-made assessments.

Great educators must be aware of these language differences and their influence on each student's academic progress. There are specific educational programs in most school districts that successfully address these students' language needs and provide ongoing professional development for teachers.

Note the Benefits of Being Standard-English Proficient—Master Communicators

Our students must become master communicators! They must fully understand the situational appropriateness of language use. Students may speak one way when they are in the lunch area, at a party, or "hangin' out" with their friends, and quite another way while in the classroom, saying a speech, or interviewing for a job.

As great teachers, you must encourage *every* English-Language Learner to develop a dual facility by engaging students in classroom activities that reinforce language skills so they can become more standard-English proficient. Check with your district to determine the language programs, trainings, and resources available for teachers to learn more regarding these strategies.

Some immediate issues related to standard-English proficiency for every child may include the following:

• **Reading**—Textbooks are written in standard English. Therefore, students who are not proficient have more difficulty processing the printed word. Comprehension and critical thinking are enhanced when students are fluent in standard English. This mandates that students possess word attack skills, core vocabulary, comprehension, and the ability to effectively use context clues to progress from basal readers to reading a variety of challenging literature, which may include poetry, folktales, plays, short stories, and novels.

• **Writing**—Generally, students write the way they speak. A discerning teacher can generally identify a paper written by a Spanish-speaking, African American, or Asian student due to nuances of word usage, grammar, and sentence structures. Greater success will be achieved by fluent standard-English speakers in their written composition skills, thus enhancing their ability to share ideas, thoughts, and feelings with a larger audience. It is also extremely important to reinforce the writing process as students are learning core content concepts and skills.

- **Test Taking**—Standardized tests are written in standard English. Students may score low on a test not because of intellectual incompetence, but rather because the language of the test is different from their own. As a classroom teacher, I have given my students sample questions from the language portion of a standardized test. After reviewing the most frequently missed items, it was my discovery that the problem areas often existed in the rules and structures of standard English.

- **College/Careers**—College is a demanding educational experience that includes term and research papers, class discussions, oral presentations, essays, examinations, debates, note taking, small-group interactions, and so forth. Professors will lecture in standard English and expect second-language students to speak and write in standard English as well. Colleges often require incoming students to complete a writing placement exam to determine their level of proficiency. In addition, many employers require potential employees to complete a writing sample describing their reasons for being qualified for the position.

Standard English is the language of the dominant society; that is, of those in power who make critical decisions affecting the lives of other people. Great educators want their students to move successfully from the classroom to the boardroom. As master communicators, they must become proficient at code switching between their home language and standard English. When the situations arise, students must know how to effectively use their standard-English skills.

Honestly, when many of our teenagers are nervous during an interview situation, there may be a tendency to speak nonstandard English if they are not already proficient.

	Example 1:	*Example 2:*
Employer:	Hello. How are you?	Hello. How are you?
Teenager:	Fine.	I am fine, thank you, and how are you?
Employer:	What is your name?	What is your name?
Teenager:	Phillip.	My name is Phillip Smith.
Employer:	Why do you want this job?	Why do you want this job?
Teenager:	I just need the money.	I want this job because it will enable me to assist my family financially and save money to further my education.
Employer:	We will be contacting you.	We will be contacting you.
Teenager:	Uh huh. Yeah. OK.	Thank you. I'll be looking forward to your call.

Take a wild guess . . . who do you think would get the job?

The following are some activities that teachers can use to promote oral communication skills for all students, especially second-language learners:

- Poetry recitations
- Storytelling (folktales)
- Speeches
- Collaborative learning groups
- Oral presentations
- Interviews
- Role playing
- Original writing presentations
- Video production
- Puppetry

- Debates
- News reporting
- Game shows
- Student-led conferences
- Oratorical contests
- Others?

True Story 2

I was at a major hospital in the pediatrics clinic "after hours" line because my son had a very bad case of the flu. A well-dressed man was standing behind me with his daughter because she also had the flu. As we began talking, he shared with me that he worked for a major corporation in the employment division. It was his responsibility to hire graduates who had been involved in a partnership program with several local inner-city high schools. He exclaimed in a very animated tone that he hated interviewing these students because they had poor standard-English skills, eye contact, and self-esteem. He said that many had very good grades, but if he were to base their employment on the interview, few of the African American or Latino teenagers would be hired. After this monologue, he asked what I did for a living. I said with a slight hesitation that I was an English teacher at one of the high schools that participated in this corporate outreach program.

From then on, I was determined to get my students ready for the real world. I had the students practice their handshakes, eye contact, posture, intonation, and standard-English skills. As a final project for this unit, I asked the students to interview one another, and I would videotape them. I also explained what would be appropriate attire for an interview. I remember a particular student, an African American male, who came from a rather poor family. He knew, however, that I had assigned this interview project to prepare the class for success in the job market. He arrived on his appointed day wearing his dad's suit, shirt, tie, and shoes. Not one student smirked or laughed when they saw these shoes, obviously designed for an old man with much larger feet. It was because of his experience with this activity that, when he graduated from high school, this same student eventually bought his own appropriate

(Continued)

(Continued)

> clothing and interviewed for and received a full-time job from the very same gentleman I had met in the hospital. The well-dressed man never knew he had hired a student from the teacher he had been chatting with in the pediatrics waiting room months prior, but I knew!

Extra Seasoning

A student's language is closely tied to his or her perception and self-esteem. It is also directly tied to his or her relationships with significant others—parents, siblings, extended family, friends, and members of the community. Teachers must honor a child's language while teaching him or her to have dual facility. This is the reality of living in a dominant society that honors standard English as the language reflecting success.

A teacher's communication can influence students' perceptions of themselves as well. It is of utmost importance for the teacher to communicate, both verbally and nonverbally, to students the message that they have the potential to be dependable, capable, and valuable.

Savory Morsel

The bad teacher's words fall on his pupils like harsh rain; the good teacher's, as gently as the dew.

—Talmud

Reflection Menu

- How do you encourage standard-English acquisition while maintaining the child's positive view of his or her first language?

- Describe the connections you make with students who come from a different racial, cultural, or linguistic background.
- How do you promote literacy in your classroom on a daily basis?

IF YOU LIKE THIS INGREDIENT, YOU'LL ALSO LIKE . . .

Ingredient 4

Ingredient 7

Praise and Self-Esteem

A Spoonful of Honey

The question has been posed: Is the glass half empty or half full? (See Figure 3.1.)

Figure 3.1   Is the Glass Half Empty or Half Full?

From an educator's point of view: Is the child half empty or half full? (See Figure 3.2.)

Figure 3.2   Is the Child Half Empty or Half Full?

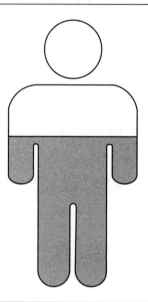

A redeeming characteristic of great teachers is that they have an optimistic view of every child they endeavor to educate!

There are pessimistic teachers who see the bad in a child:

- Johnny, you didn't bring any paper!
- Johnny, you're late again!
- Johnny, you only have one pencil!
- Johnny, you failed your math test . . . for the second time!

There are optimistic teachers who see the good in a child:

- Johnny, you brought your notebook; now please bring your paper tomorrow.
- Johnny, you were on time yesterday and I was very pleased. Let's continue to arrive on time!
- Johnny, you got an A in vocabulary and a B in science; now let's use that same great mind to bring up your math grade.

It's amazing what outcomes a teacher can produce by consistently using praise with children. It absolutely works wonders! Johnny is not all bad!

Reinforcing the Positive Attributes of Students

Each of us has been created with positive attributes. As great educators, it is essential to identify each child's qualities and create situations that will reinforce the good ones and continue the development of those that need improvement. Whenever you have students who are lacking in a particular area, try focusing on the positive first, then assist them with what needs improvement. This diminishes negative feelings and resentment between the student and teacher, and likely enhances the teamwork between the two.

If a teacher makes a negative comment in front of a student's peers, you can bet that the student's wall of defensive behavior and conversation will immediately go up! Students also lose respect for a teacher who treats them in a disrespectful manner, especially in front of their peers!

Remember, you are the adult . . . your courteous, calm, and respectful behavior should be the perpetual "flavor of the day." Even when a child has made you angry or upset . . . you have to "take the high road." It's very difficult, I know, but most children will eventually apologize for their behavior (in one way or another) when they know that their teacher has dealt with them honestly, maturely, and fairly. It also achieves your ultimate goal to be a positive role model not only for this particular student but also for the entire class, which is closely scrutinizing how you have reacted in a tough situation and trusted that they will also emulate your genuine qualities!

No respect! No progress! For this very reason, therefore, consistently use praise during each student's tenure in your classroom. It really does enhance each child's self-esteem!

A child can . . . because he believes he can.

A child believes he can . . . because you believe he can.

Some important considerations:

- Teacher expectations are crucial in a successful classroom.
- Set your standards high!
- Challenge your students to soar toward a high level of excellence.
- Don't allow them to quit or give up.
- Never let them say "I can't."
- Remember that academic performance is not solely influenced by ethnicity, demographics, or socioeconomic status. The teacher's qualifications and expertise are critical factors as well.
- Students are willing to try new things, take risks, and actively participate in class and extracurricular activities when they feel a sense of positive self-worth in a trusting learning environment.
- As a great teacher, you should individually assess each student's skills to further develop his or her inherent abilities, develop those unmastered skills, and tailor your lessons to promote his or her abilities.

Praise lubricates the machinery that propels learners toward mountain-top experiences!

True Story

I saw a student who had graduated from high school four years prior. She told me how she matriculated to college on a full four-year academic scholarship and graduated at the top of her class. All through college, she relayed joyfully with her classmates how she kept remembering that her English teacher (yours truly) encouraged her "never to give up, never say 'I can't,' and never settle for second best."

Now she was looking forward to a fully paid scholarship to graduate school and was determined to reach her goal to climb the proverbial corporate ladder. She always knew that no matter how difficult the challenge, giving up was never an option!

I waited until after we said our good-byes, and I walked in an almost trance-like state back to my car. For a long while, I just sat there and wept softly because I knew that many of these precious students do indeed grow up to be responsible and successful adults. I was so sure that constantly giving them praise was an important factor to build their self-esteem and assurance that they could march to the beat of their own drum. I felt so absolutely blessed that I was allowed to play a small part in this musical medley called life!

To touch a child's life supercedes academics; it reaches into the very essence of a human being—mind, body, and soul. It influences a student's formative years, teenage years, and adulthood, including his or her relationships and self-perceptions. The pure ecstasy of teaching is that the good you do will always return to you bountifully. It is so far-reaching to comprehend that the type of influence a child receives in one year in my classroom can last for his or her entire lifetime. I am awed and humbled to be in such a divine position to inspire and educate young people and the contagious effect they have on everyone around them.

A marvelous self-esteem builder is to have students recite poetry, pledges, proverbs, lyrics, or affirmations each day. Make this a part of your daily agenda. It has proven to have a powerful impact on both elementary and secondary students.

Suggestions for positive extrinsic reinforcements may also include the following:

- Pats on the back
- Leadership roles
- Stickers
- Awards
- Certificates

- Plaques
- Field trips
- Calls home
- Complimentary notices
- Student of the month awards
- Most-improved student awards
- Assignments on display
- Features in the class or school newsletter
- Stars or happy faces on students' papers
- Reward "bucks"

In addition, use words, phrases, or sentences of praise when appropriate during your conversations with students each day. They should leave your classroom feeling a sense of accomplishment and empowerment—ready to take on the world!

It is also important to note that students' ultimate success should be based on their intrinsic values. In other words, students should exhibit behaviors and skills that promote their own academic abilities because they value the personal satisfaction of doing well. Their behaviors are not merely based on receiving some type of token from their teacher or parent. Students who are driven to succeed for their own self-satisfaction generally make greater strides toward both short- and long-term achievements.

The following are 50 expressions of praise and encouragement. You may have some others that you find may enhance your students' self-esteem. Add them to this list and share them with your colleagues.

Great	Good thinking
Fantastic	A great accomplishment
A scholar	Marvelous
Hooray	Always do your best
Genius at work	Put on your thinking cap

You're unique	Super
Keep up the good work	A star is born!
There are no failures	Getting better with each try
Stupendous	Never use the word *can't*
A great effort	Sensational
It gets better every day	You're improving
I'm proud of you	I'm glad you thought of that
Outstanding	Sky's the limit
Never say never	Good work
Brilliant	That's wonderful
Genius	A good try
Very creative	Keep trying
A great idea	A valiant effort
Bravo	That's a winner
Incredible	Excellent
Best in the West	Impressive
Fine job	You're one in a million
Masterful	The best I've seen yet
You are very smart	Good answer
Superb	Wow

Extra Seasoning

Praise is what we do! It influences the intellectual, emotional, and spiritual well-being of your students. A candle does not lose its light by lighting another candle!

Savory Morsel

All of us need to convey to our students and our colleagues every day that "you are important to me as a person."

—Harry and Rosemary Wong (1998, p. 65)

Reflection Menu

- How can you attach words of praise to specific tasks or activities that your students have completed?
- Consider the frequency of your praise to all of the children in your room—boys, girls, special needs, minority, gifted, talkative, truant.
- Describe how your learning environment exhibits evidence of equity, fairness, risk taking, and belonging.

If You Like This Ingredient, You'll Also Like . . .

Ingredient 1

Ingredient 5

INGREDIENT 4

Respect and Self-Respect

Marinating Positive Relationships

MAINTAINING RESPECTFUL BEHAVIOR IN THE CLASSROOM

In many ways, we have allowed our youngsters to become lax in displaying respectful behavior in the classroom as well as on the school grounds. We need to get back to the basics, that is, to the "meat and potatoes" of respectful behavior.

Many teachers will insist that this is not their job: "That's what the parents are supposed to do." Well, yes, they are vital contributors. But these young people spend six to eight hours each day at school. It certainly wouldn't hurt for teachers to put forth some effort too! The amazing thing is that it really does not take much additional time from your already hectic schedule to reinforce these skills. The great benefit is that it will positively affect the students in such areas as self-esteem, discipline, leadership, and more.

This area of socialization encourages students to enter and exit a classroom, conduct conversations, and attend field trips, assemblies, and other social activities with all of the appropriate protocols.

Let's think of words and phrases that reflect social amenities and common courtesies:

- "Excuse me"
- "Pardon me"
- "May I?"
- "Thank you"
- "I apologize"
- "Yes/No, Mr. or Ms. Teacher"

If you are speaking to someone, for example, and a student needs to say something, then he or she can follow a designated protocol. The student can learn that it is important that he or she not interrupt the teacher's conversation, but rather say, "Excuse me." Then he or she needs to wait for an appropriate break in your conversation or for you to pause in your conversation to address the student. This is true of all ages. Teenagers need encouragement to use these social amenities just like little children!

TEACHERS CAN MODEL RESPECT AND SELF-RESPECT

Teachers can absolutely model respect and self-respect during class time and throughout the school day. Students are not always aware when they are exhibiting behaviors that are "rough around the edges," and their daily encounters with teachers and peers can afford them the opportunity to practice these appropriate behaviors. It is clear that teachers must start with themselves, by modeling respectful behaviors as they engage with colleagues and students. Eventually, this will become a natural part of your daily encounters with the students and their encounters with one another. Remember that these students will matriculate from preschool through high school. After graduation, they will seek employment or attend college (or both), and they need to develop these social skills, which may mean the difference between being hired for a job or satisfactorily completing an interview for college entrance or not.

Here are suggestions for teachers who want to support the development of students' social skills (add your own creative ideas to this list):

- Depending on the culture of your school, ask young men to take off their hats as soon as they enter a classroom. Even the monitors from other classes or offices should be required to follow this rule. I have often heard young men advising one another, "Man, that's Ms. Moultrie Turner, and you have to take your hat off when you go into *her* classroom." *Special Note:* In many schools, hats are not even allowed on school campuses because of their potential for association with certain gangs.

- When appropriate, ask a young man entering a door at the same time as a young lady to allow her to enter first.

- If your class is expecting a guest, ask a responsible young man or young woman to serve as the guest's escort from the office to the classroom. Review appropriate procedures for greeting guests beforehand. Rehearse an introduction, such as, "Good morning, Mr./Ms. _____. My name is _____. I will be escorting you to Ms. Moultrie Turner's class." Then the student should walk through the hallways at the same pace as the guest. While on the way to class, engage the guest in a light conversation, for example, by citing interesting facts about the campus.

- Review with students the appropriate manner to walk into the auditorium during an assembly. You may also explain to the students the difference between applauding in a fine arts auditorium compared with in a stadium at a sporting event.

- Explain to students the appropriate dress for attendance at an opera, ballet, or theater performance, while attending a school-sponsored field trip.

True Story 1

I was a teaching assistant in an inner-city middle school of predominantly African American and Latino students. Their English teacher planned an evening field trip to the opera in a beautiful auditorium in downtown Oakland, California. She arrived in an after-five sequined dress and a fur coat. I was also dressed up appropriately in a fancy outfit. The students, however, arrived in jeans, T-shirts, jackets, baseball caps, tennis shoes, and whatever else a teenager would commonly wear. They were angry, embarrassed, and disappointed that their teacher had not explained to them what they should have worn to the opera. The students almost refused to board the bus and felt betrayed by their teacher because they felt that she did not adequately prepare them for this outing. I felt bad for them because I assumed that the teacher had explained the appropriate dress for the opera, since I only worked in her classroom three days per week. This experience definitely left a lasting impression on me, and I always made it a part of my conversations with my own students when I eventually became a full-time teacher.

Many of these amenities contribute in important ways to student successes in leadership roles, college and job interviews, personal relationships, character development, and discipline. Teaching social amenities is a very small price to pay for such valuable and far-reaching rewards in each of your students' lives.

True Story 2

I had a young man in my high school class who really took to heart his responsibility for helping female peers and teachers. Prior to being enrolled in my class, this young man was known for being very abrupt, sometimes downright unkind, and he displayed a pretty bad temper once in a while. He was unconcerned about other people's feelings and invested little time trying to understand that his words and actions were adversely affecting other people.

At first, he totally resisted this whole notion that he was to conduct himself like a gentleman and make sure that his words and behavior coincided with this new approach to dealing with others. Gradually, he began to make the connection between his kind acts and people responding to him in a kind way as well. In addition to his interpersonal skills, this young man's grades improved and his other teachers actually began to look forward to his arrival in their class each day.

A complete transformation occurred when this same student took it upon himself to wait in the hallway just outside the main office where the teachers signed in and picked up their mail in the morning. If he saw one of his female teachers with a lot of papers or books in her hand, he would offer to assist by carrying her belongings to the classroom. After the shock wore off, the teachers often questioned him about his new attitude. He explained to each teacher that I was reinforcing etiquette skills in my classroom. I was affectionately teased about it by many of my colleagues, but they were sure happy that this gruff young man had become such a gentle giant!

Extra Seasoning

Social skills and etiquette should be woven into the fabric of each child's educational experience.

Savory Morsel

Our looks play an important part in the construction of our attitude.

—John C. Maxwell (2003, p. 40)

Reflection Menu

- What types of social behaviors do you consider to be acceptable in your classroom?
- How might you reinforce these skills in your classroom?

- What role do you directly play to ensure that these behaviors are consistently displayed?

IF YOU LIKE THIS INGREDIENT, YOU'LL ALSO LIKE . . .

Ingredient 1

Ingredient 2

Classroom Environment

An Equitable Dining Room

The environment of the classroom plays a crucial role in the success of the classroom. Every teacher, whether elementary or secondary, must creatively design a multisensory classroom because it provides an environment that motivates students to learn. Colors should be appealing, but not too bright. After all, we want the children to be energized by the colors on the walls, not bouncing off the walls!

CREATE A WARM AND TRUSTING COMMUNITY OF LEARNERS

It is important that each teacher spends the first week of school establishing a "community of learners," whereby students embrace the concept that everyone is unique, yet each student is integral to the functioning and success of the entire group. "Getting to know you" activities might include interviewing one another, name games, designing a personal poster of one's attributes, creating a poem using student names, drawing self-portraits, or writing personal notes to the teacher or a classmate. Great teachers must purposely and regularly design and organize activities that promote collaborative learning and celebrate this strong and productive learning environment throughout the school year.

Children of all ages need to feel that they are safe in your room. It must be safe for them to take risks, accept challenges, make mistakes, experience setbacks, ask questions, and reveal dilemmas and triumphs. A great teacher will establish a trusting, communicative, and honest relationship with each student and create an environment that promotes these attributes among all students for the entire school year.

A classroom must be founded on trust and a community of learners who are committed to the best within themselves and who can also reasonably expect these same behaviors from the other students in the room.

Your Classroom Belongs to Everyone

It is essential that you communicate clearly and consistently with your students that the classroom belongs to everyone. I know that you and your students are extremely busy, but it is important to slow down and spend some time maintaining a clean, organized, and comfortable room environment. Doing this communicates to students that the classroom belongs to everyone, and therefore, everyone has to assist with its upkeep. You can assign classroom monitors, or you can ask all of the students to stop three to five minutes before recess, lunch, or dismissal to pick up paper, straighten the desks, stack instructional materials, empty the trash, put magazines or books back on the shelves, and so on. You should not do this all by yourself.

Believe me, an administrator is not going to be able to concentrate on an observation or evaluation in your class if he or she first has to step over trash on the floor or go around your desk piled high with books and papers. Even if you present an excellent lesson, a messy room will definitely leave a lasting impression!

Your Classroom Is a Multisensory Environment

Bulletin boards or display tables may include any or all of the following:

- District or state content standards
- School or classroom motto, mission, or vision
- Announcements
- Birthdays
- Projects
- Performance tasks or culminating tasks
- Essays, poems, or term papers
- Arts and crafts
- Visuals reflecting literature currently being taught, for example:
  - *Charlotte's Web*: farm animals, barn, spider
  - *The Scarlet Letter:* colonial clothing, letter "A," scaffold

- Charts, pictures, posters, murals
- Students' work samples
- Rubrics and scoring guides
- School bulletins, newspaper clippings, upcoming events
- Class song or poem
- School or class rules or standards of behavior
- Learning centers
- Computer centers or labs
- Photos, for example:
  - Student of the week
  - Student of the month
  - Most-improved student

- Reading corner: magazines, novels, comic books, newspapers
- Current events

- Word wall
- Celebrations of diversity
- Connections between content areas

Special Note: Teachers may want to add a small sofa, a rocking or lounge chair, a lamp, plants, or a collage of pictures of past and present students to make the classroom an inclusive place.

It is also great to have classical music playing softly in the background.

Visual displays should aim to teach more than one skill. Let's take a peek into a lower elementary classroom's environment. In an alphabet display on the bulletin board or wall, for example, imagine the letters "A" and "a" with a vivid picture of an apple (each corresponding letter would follow suit) that may include any or all of the following:

- Uppercase letter
- Lowercase letter
- Classification, such as fruit
- Colors, such as red, green, yellow
- Apples grown on trees
- Apples grown on a farm
- Apples bought in the produce section at the market
- Pronunciation of "a"
- Words that begin with "a"
- Short vowel "a"
- Other short vowel "a" words
- Weight of apples
- Use of a scale
- Metric versus pounds
- Numbers (How many apples?)
- Estimation (How many apples are in the barrel?)

The room environment in a secondary classroom could include the following:

- Math
  o Steps to solve equations
  o Dimensions, shapes

- o Charts and graphs
- o Content literacy

- Science
  - o Life cycles
  - o Elements chart
  - o Scientific process
  - o Content literacy

- Social studies
  - o Famous leaders
  - o Historical timelines or events
  - o World wars
  - o Content literacy

- Language arts
  - o Literary terms
  - o Genres
  - o Writing process
  - o Readers and writers workshops

One of the ways that a great teacher can capture the theme of a unit or lesson is by clearly making connections between the lessons or activities and the learning environment. A multisensory classroom goes a long way in encouraging a community of learners to feel a sense of belonging, because the room reflects who they are as lifelong learners.

It is important that students take an active role in creating the learning environment associated with the teacher's units, lessons, or content standards. Design a rain forest, colonial settlement, animal habitat, igloo, volcano, national monument, or one of the seven wonders of the world right in your own classroom. They can learn and have fun at the same time . . . what a concept!

Students learn so much when they can make the connection between content areas, lessons, and hands-on activities. It is also a great idea to take the students on a field trip, go on summer schoolwide or grade-level outings, or ask students to bring primary sources from trips they have enjoyed with their families and include these realia in your visual displays and class discussions.

It is important to note that when you place student work on display in the classroom, avoid posting handouts or dittos. Rather, use authentic work samples that represent the students' creativity, intellect, critical thinking, and ingenuity.

SEATING ARRANGEMENTS AND STUDENT ROLES INFLUENCE THE ENVIRONMENT

In Figures 5.1 and 5.2, notice the shaded area in the front of the classroom, which I call the teacher's Power Position. Initially, as you are establishing clear delineations of authority, it is a clear, nonverbal message to the students that *you* are in charge of your classroom.

In addition to your Power Position, the teacher must put key players in strategic locations. These key players are usually the students who are conscientious, diligent, and highly motivated. They can also include those students with high energy, but who are possibly performing below their abilities. It is not uncommon to see these students, once assigned a leadership role, become more organized, attentive, and productive. Quite frankly, every child should eventually have some sort of leadership role in your classroom during the school year. It definitely creates a culture of mutual respect, dependence, and camaraderie.

Adjustments can be made in the seating arrangement during special class projects, cooperative learning, and presentations. Teachers may rearrange the seats into a circular arrangement during specific activities, for example, to give students an opportunity to communicate with one another face to face. This can heighten communication, teamwork, and the appreciation developed for the skills and talents each student brings to the classroom and potentially reduce conflicts that may exist among students.

I would highly recommend that you set up your desk or table arrangement in a way that lends itself to allow students daily dialogue with one another. This can include desks that support opportunities for a pair-share, triad, quads, or cooperative learning groups. It is when students discuss or teach one another issues or concepts that teachers can assess their higher levels of cognition. Remember that learning is a social activity. Lecturing has far less impact on learning than allowing students the opportunity to engage in meaningful dialogue with one another.

Remember also that your students will not learn much if the environment is disrupted by a few students. Disruptive students should not dictate how much of your lesson will be successfully completed in a given day for the majority of the students. Those few students need to get with the program!

An absolute no-no is to turn the students' desks facing the door. This causes the students to be more interested in what is going on outside than what you are teaching in the classroom! With your back to the door, you may leave yourself open to unmonitored and unwanted visitations of students who may not fully respect the fact that you are trying to teach your class. This also has the potential to invite mischief or unforeseen danger. It is always better to be safe than sorry!

RESPECT IS THE DISH OF THE DAY . . . EVERY DAY

There are restaurants that serve a variety of very tasty dishes but are frequented by patrons because of their specialty dishes. People come from far and wide to have that particularly scrumptious dish. In fact, it is word of mouth by previously satisfied customers that promotes the reputation of a well-known restaurant. The same is true of your classroom. It is not enough to have an absolutely gorgeous physical environment. More important, students (and their parents) are looking for teachers who have an inviting, loving, respectful, heart-to-heart learning environment. This is the kind of classroom that makes students feel great when they leave your room, talk about your class affectionately to their parents, and

Figure 5.1 Aerial View of Classroom

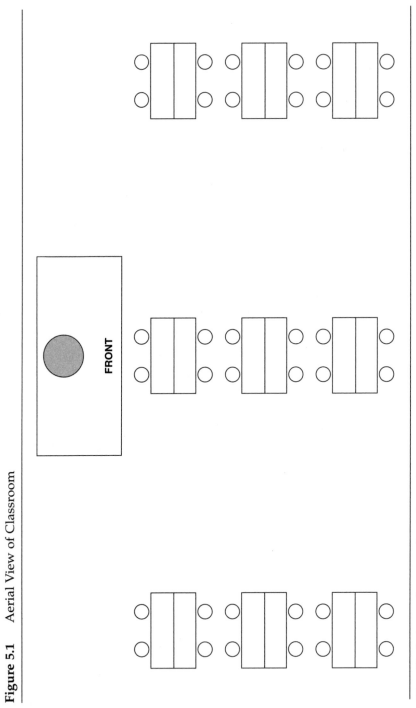

FRONT

Note: Shaded area shows teacher's Power Position.

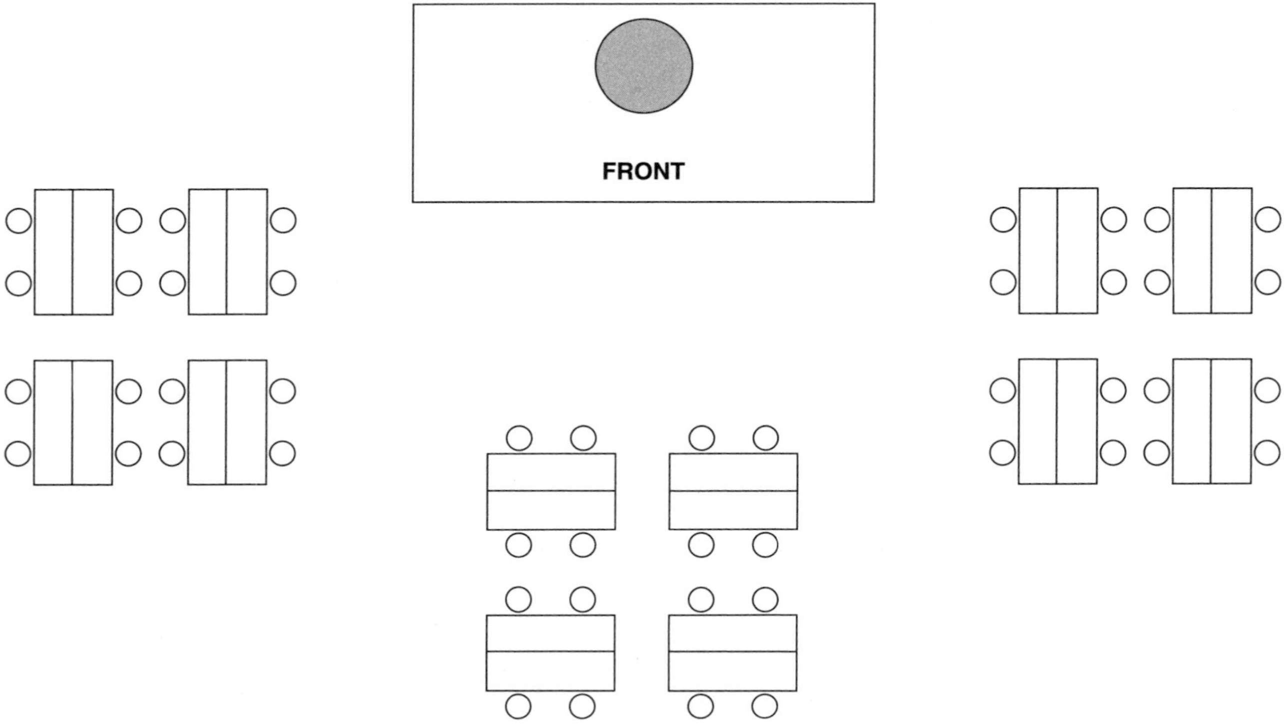

Figure 5.2 Aerial View of Classroom: Note How Seating Arrangements and Student Roles Influence the Environment

get up in the morning anxiously anticipating the time when they can return to your sanctuary of learning and edification.

A great teacher purposely provides opportunities for student ownership in the classroom. If the students see it as their classroom, then they are more likely to take responsibility in showing pride and respect for every stakeholder.

The room environment, therefore, is not just the physical environment, but it includes the ambiance of the classroom as well. A learning community does not happen by accident. As a great teacher, you must purposely design it by how you treat students, how you allow students to treat one another, how you welcome a new student to your class, how you and your students treat visitors, and how problems are resolved and everyone is treated with respect and dignity. Students must take ownership for the learning environment and their consistent and meaningful participation. It must be the dish of the day . . . all of the ingredients that are sure to lure the satisfied customer back to your classroom day after day. There are classrooms that some students dread going to each day and others that students have an insatiable appetite to attend because they are having a satisfying and well-balanced academic experience.

Which one of these best fits the description of your classroom?

IT'S A SHAME TO WASTE . . . ANYTHING!

When I was growing up, my mother used to insist that I ate everything on my plate, even if it was something that I did not particularly like to eat. She would remind me that there were starving children in developing countries who would love to eat the very thing that I was sure needed to be cast into the abyss of forgetfulness or at least the nearest trash can! She would adamantly declare that "waste was shameful."

Likewise, I challenge you as great teachers not to waste students' instructional time. It is too precious, and children deserve to be nourished with well-balanced and well-organized lessons or activities. The learning environment also involves how effectively you and your students master the use of instructional time. It is too important to waste!

True Story

I visited a new teacher who worked with middle-school urban youth. He sent many students out of the class daily as a disciplinary measure, and the grades of these students were extremely low. I observed this teacher with his prior approval, and the day and time were prearranged. When I walked into his classroom, I was horrified to see that there was so much trash on the floor that I almost needed knee-high rubber boots to wade through the debris to get to the rear of the classroom where there were vacant seats. There was absolutely no student work on the chalkboard, and there were no bulletin boards, displays, or subject-specific visuals on the walls. In fact, if I did not know the subject this teacher taught prior to my visit, I would not have been able to determine the subject solely from looking around his room. (He was a social studies teacher.)

During my 30-minute observation, most of the students were a bit unruly, and many paid very little attention to the teacher. One student in the rear of the classroom threw his candy wrapper on the floor. Then he turned to a friend and humorously chuckled that the teacher would never know that he was the culprit since his paper only added to those of previous offenders.

During our post-conference, I explained to the teacher that he might experience fewer discipline problems if his room environment unequivocally bespoke to students as they crossed the threshold of his classroom that this was a place of business— the business of learning! This teacher and his students spent several weeks organizing and decorating the classroom. Together, they created a room environment that made history and their desire to learn come alive!

EXTRA SEASONING

Students will learn in leaps and bounds when there is an environment that celebrates them as unique, talented, intelligent, and creative people. This includes the physical environment as well as the trusting, loving, and respectful culture of the classroom. As a great teacher, make sure that these important ingredients are served fresh daily.

Savory Morsel

Environment plays a critical role in the classroom. How you set up your room affects the learning that will take place. . . . Environment means more than the furniture arrangement.

—Moran, Stobbe, Baron, Miller, and
Moir (2000, pp. 17–18)

Reflection Menu

- How does your room environment support learning for all of your students?
- Consider the variety of ways that student work is displayed in your classroom.
- How do you encourage your students to be excited about arriving in your classroom each day and considering themselves a viable member of the learning community?

If You Like This Ingredient, You'll Also Like . . .

Ingredient 3

Ingredient 11

Classroom Management

A Great Teacher Is the Master Chef

A great teacher considers his or her classroom management system to be an absolutely essential ingredient from the very first day of school. According to Harry and Rosemary Wong (1998), what you do during the first days of school will determine your success or failure for the rest of the school year. A teacher will either win or lose his or her class during the very first days of school.

In fact, Wong and Wong further state that the rules and procedures that a teacher establishes and consistently reinforces from the first day of school will prove to make the difference in the classroom. Student achievement at the end of the year is directly related to the degree to which the teacher establishes good management of classroom procedures in the very first week of school. An excellent teacher/manager takes into consideration the students, time, space, and materials simultaneously to ensure a well-managed classroom.

Set Clear Guidelines, Rules, and Procedures

As strange as it may seem, students actually want their teachers to be clear about the classroom guidelines, rules, and procedures for appropriate conduct, no matter what age or grade. This is true for elementary, middle, and high school students. They want to know the parameters for what is acceptable and what is unacceptable in the classroom.

Many discipline problems can often be directly associated with the teacher's failure to set clear and doable rules and procedures. It is important to note that there should be no more than five or six classroom rules, which are simple and clear, and which everyone in the classroom can live with.

Here is an example:

Classroom Rules

1. Listen carefully.

2. Follow directions.

3. Work quietly. Do not disturb others who are working.

4. Work and play safely.

5. Respect yourself, others, personal property, and school.

To avoid many potential disruptions or behavior problems, a great teacher sets up procedures that will ensure that the classroom is run efficiently. A partial list of some important procedures may include the following:

- Being absent
- Being tardy
- Interrupting
- Asking questions during class discussion
- Being excused to the restroom, office, or extracurricular activities

- Retrieving a book from bookshelves or cabinets
- Walking in the classroom after the class had begun
- Submitting assignments
- Turning in late work or make-up work
- Getting one's pencil sharpened
- Passing out or collecting materials
- Rotating to centers, such as reading, writing, mathematics, listening, computers
- Retrieving balls and jump ropes for recess (for elementary grades)
- Cleaning up
- Being dismissed

INGREDIENTS FOR RUNNING AN EFFECTIVE CLASSROOM

When it comes to the business of running an effective classroom, the teacher is just like the master chef who considers not only the most qualified employees and their specialty dishes, but also the daily purchases to maintain fresh ingredients; proper pots, pans, and utensils; and adequate spices, seasonings, and garnishments. Likewise, a teacher must consider every aspect of his or her classroom and purposely design procedures that will create a flavorful classroom that allows everyone to interact effectively and design a management system that ensures the success of all students.

Greet the Students at the Door of the Classroom

Beginning on the first day of school and throughout the year, I encourage every teacher to stand at the door of his or her classroom and greet students as they enter. A warm smile, a hello, and a compliment or praiseworthy comment as students cross the threshold of your door set a positive tone for the rest of the school day and school year.

Post the Class Agenda

Students perform well when their day is structured and organized. One of the ways I make sure this is built into the daily procedures is by writing an agenda on the board. When students walk into your classroom, they should be able to see exactly what the school day or class period will include by having it written visibly on the board.

Sample Agenda for an Elementary Classroom

Elementary teachers can designate the time for the activities for the entire day, for example:

8:00 A.M.–10:00 A.M.	Language arts
10:00 A.M.–10:15 A.M.	Recess
10:15 A.M.–12:00 P.M.	Mathematics
12:00 P.M.–12:30 P.M.	Lunch
12:30 P.M.–2:15 P.M.	Social studies, science, fine arts, physical education

Make adjustments in the use of time as deemed necessary.

Sample Agenda for a Secondary Classroom
With Traditional Schedule (55 Minutes)

Secondary classrooms can structure their agenda for each class period since they generally have five class periods of approximately 55 minutes each. It will take a little extra time on your part, but I highly recommend that you place a different agenda on the board for each "preparation." If you do not have the board space, write the agenda on chart paper and post it or use transparencies on an overhead projector.

- Dispatch/warm up (7 minutes)
  - Roll

- Announcements (5 minutes)
  o Collect homework
- Review information from previous class sessions (10 minutes)
- Directed lesson (10 minutes)
- Guided group practice or independent work (10 minutes)
- Summarize/Q&A (5 minutes)
- Introduce homework (5 minutes)
- Clean up (3 minutes)

Make adjustments in the use of time as deemed necessary.

Sample Agenda for a Secondary
Classroom With Block Schedule (90 Minutes)

Some secondary schools use a block schedule allowing for more instructional time; therefore, it is vital for these teachers to organize their time to avoid discipline problems, maintain student engagement, and make good use of this extended instructional time.

- Dispatch/warm up (10 minutes)
  o Roll
- Announcements (5 minutes)
  o Collect homework
- Review information from previous class sessions (10 minutes)
  o Q&A
- Directed lesson (10 minutes)
- Guided group practice (15 minutes)
  o Cooperative learning groups
  o Role playing
  o Debates
  o Group discussion
  o Projects
- Independent work (15 minutes)

- Summarize/Q&A (10 minutes)
- Introduce homework (10 minutes)
- Clean up (5 minutes)

Make adjustments in the use of time as deemed necessary.

Post a Warm-Up Activity

While the teacher is taking roll and handling other administrative business, elementary and secondary students should be given a warm-up activity such as a journal or dispatch assignment. It is most effective to have the dispatch either review information from previous class lessons or as a tickler for the lesson of the day. The topic should already be written on the board or on the overhead projector when students enter the classroom. Students should have a composition book or designated place in their notebook for entering and completing the warm-up each day.

Set Up Headings for Papers

Students should also be required to set up the heading on their papers in preparation for the directed lesson, which will begin after they have completed the warm-up activity. Every assignment in my class had a title, which made grading, record keeping, and returning papers easier and more efficient. In fact, it is a good idea to display an enlargement of a correct paper set up and headings for easy reference by the students. I highly recommend that departments agree on a heading format so that students have continuity from one teacher to the next and one subject to the next (see Figure 6.1).

Possible Warm-Up Activities for Elementary Classrooms

Elementary students may be assigned journal entries that describe current or upcoming events. The journal or dispatch entries can also reinforce fundamental reading, writing, or math skills. The following is a sample of possibilities:

Figure 6.1   Sample Headings for Assignments

Name: (last, first)	
Date:	
Subject:	
Title of Assignment:	

- Days of the week
- Months of the year
- Alphabet
- Numbers
- Colors
- Shapes
- Vocabulary
- Language
- Mathematics
- Seasons
- Parts of speech
- Critical thinking
- Creative writing

Possible Warm-Up Activities for Secondary Classrooms

For secondary students, dispatch or journal ideas may involve the following ideas:

- Hypothetical situations:
  - If I won a million dollars, I would . . .
  - If I could go anywhere in the world, I would . . .
  - If I were the president of the United States of America, I would . . .
  - If I could make a positive change in the world, it would be . . .
  - If I could meet anyone famous, it would be . . .
  - If I could choose any profession, it would be . . .

- Proverbs: cultural; interpreting wisdom (available in local library or bookstore)
- Current events: Choose a headline story or a controversy that is political, social, economic, racial, global, etc.
- Brainteasers: math, science, economics, geography, language arts, etc.
- Quotations: Interpret their meanings, express opinions, etc.
- *The Book of Questions* (Stock, 1987): Moral or ethical dilemmas, justifying choices, etc.
- Content area skills
- Literacy skills

Students of all ages perform well using this warm-up approach, because there is a sense of getting down to business as soon as they enter the room. Students understand clearly that there is no time for fooling around when it comes to their learning. Education is a serious matter and requires the diligence and commitment of everyone from the beginning of the day or class period to the very end: bell-to-bell instruction.

Sustained Silent Reading (SSR)

Teachers may choose to give students an opportunity during class time to select reading materials—magazines, novels, comic books, newspapers—and read quietly for 10 to 15 minutes. SSR may also include the students keeping a log, graphic organizer, or summary of their readings. This can be an activity every day or two to three times each week, while alternating with a dispatch or journal. Many schools use either homeroom or advisory as an optimal time to promote SSR as a schoolwide activity.

Create Smooth Transitions

Now that the students have completed the dispatch, journal, and SSR and you have taken roll, it is time to transition to the next activity. As an excellent classroom manager, remember that the agenda you wrote on the board should consider the required transition time in the planning. Suggestions for avoiding lost time while transitioning between activities include the following:

- Designating a "time monitor"
- Using an egg timer
- Using an overhead projector timer—set it on the overhead and the time projects onto the screen
- Using a small bell, chime, or musical instrument
- Raising a hand
- Raising five fingers and counting down 5-4-3-2-1

I don't recommend flashing the lights. This can be bad for the eyes or possibly cause seizures.

But be careful—don't become overzealous! There may (and should) be times when class discussions, activities, or projects extend past the designated time on your agenda. A teachable moment may require that you divert from the lesson to take full advantage of a content-related question, thought, or idea. When the "ahas" happen, the "lightbulbs" go on, and your students want to explore a concept further through extended classroom discussions, relax! There is great value in spontaneity. But you knew that already, right?

It is also important to remember that an effective classroom environment (see Ingredient 5) is closely connected to classroom management. When the students move from their warm-up activity to directed teaching, classroom discussion, cooperative learning, independent study, or centers, the teacher should have already taken into consideration and planned for resource materials, books, equipment, and the alternate arrangement of tables and chairs.

Before transitioning students, make sure that you clearly explain the next lesson or activity, objectives, or procedures and briefly entertain any pertinent questions. This will allow the students to get started immediately without wasting precious time still trying to figure out their assignment once they get into groups. As soon as they are in place, you want your students to be able to focus on the task at hand. You should not exhaust your time attempting to move around the classroom trying to explain the task to individual students another 20 times because your students did not understand the charge the first time.

Provide Enrichment Activities for Early Finishers

Always make allowances for those students who may finish early during their independent practice and could potentially cause an interruption to the other students in your class who are not quite done. We do not want these students to become disruptive because they are bored or impatient. Sometimes they are done early because they did not thoroughly complete the assignment as you have specified. Other times, students are done and need an extended activity. Please do not designate them as teaching assistants who walk around the room helping you to engage the "less motivated" pupils—that is not their job. Instead, provide enrichment activities, such as the computer center, math manipulatives, reading corner, or projects that will further heighten their learning. Although peer teaching has valid outcomes, it is important that you use discretion.

Likewise, be sure to design your lessons and room environment to ensure the inclusion of any special-needs students so that they will also experience academic success and acceptance in the classroom. This could also be a great time for those teachers who have the luxury of a resource teacher to possibly have him or her work with a small group of students with specific yet similar learning needs, while you work with the remainder of the class or vice versa.

Clean Up and Dismissal

Once you complete the activities planned for the day, make sure that you leave some time, possibly three to five minutes, at the end of the class for necessary housekeeping tasks with the assistance of your designated student monitors (remember to rotate these roles). These tasks may include the following:

- Clean up work areas
- Return desks to original order (if necessary)
- Return books or other resource materials
- Turn off the computers or save information on disks
- Summarize the day's lesson and address briefly the next day's challenges
- Collect classwork
- Explain homework
- Distribute school newsletters or any other communication to parents
- Gather backpacks, straighten desks, and collect personal belongings
- Praise the students for specific achievements of the day

Congratulations! You have successfully completed your instructional day.

Now you can see how a well-managed classroom directly influences your effectiveness as a great teacher!

True Story

As English Department chairperson, I made a point to visit classrooms of the other teachers in my department. One day, I visited a particular class and was absolutely shocked to find that approximately 28 students were present in class, but only five or six students were attentive to the lesson being taught. It took all the self-control I could muster to stay in my seat and not jump on the chair and yell at the top of my lungs:

"Hey, can't you see that your students aren't listening?"

Through a reflective conversation later the same day, I asked the teacher what he felt about the lesson executed during my "planned" visit. I chose my words wisely and described what

(Continued)

(Continued)

I observed during my visit. I noticed that five to six students were listening, three girls were applying makeup, five students were engaged in their own conversations, two students were asleep, three students had on headphones with music playing, many students' textbooks were closed, one student was doodling on the desk, and a few students walked out of the back door without his knowledge or permission!

His reply was, "Yes, all that may be true, but the five or six students who were paying attention will do well on my test this Friday!"

Extra Seasoning

You communicate to students that you care about them by the way you organize and manage their day. It says to them that you value their time, energy, and academic growth and you will honor them by planning a day that is challenging, interesting, and relevant.

Savory Morsel

Anything that you do not structure to your advantage, someone else will structure to their advantage.

—Fred Jones (2000)

Reflection Menu

- What are the top five rules you think are important in your classroom?
- How clear are your procedures for creating an organized and well-run classroom?

- What areas in classroom management need improvement, and what changes will you make to ensure that these improvements are successfully executed?

IF YOU LIKE THIS INGREDIENT, YOU'LL ALSO LIKE . . .

Ingredient 7

Ingredient 8

Discipline

Making Sure the Cake Rises

Once I heard a great administrator say to his staff, "There is a difference between authority and power. The ideal is that a teacher has both. Unfortunately, it is possible to have one and not the other. For example, as a teacher you are the *authority,* but if your students all walk out of the room, they have the *power!*"

WHO IS IN CONTROL OF YOUR CLASSROOM?

The following are some proven strategies that should be implemented from the first day of school to ensure their success:

- Establish a professional, cordial, and respectful relationship with your students at the onset of a new school year. It is important that you establish clear expectations and parameters for a positive learning community.
- Engage the students during the first week of school in "getting to know you" types of activities so there is a sense of camaraderie or community among all of your students. It is important to engage in these types of activities throughout the school year as well.

- Refer to yourself in personal terms, so they understand that you are not an uncaring and unfeeling robot. Students need to know that teachers are people whose profession is teaching. Yes, you are an individual with a family, outside commitments, emotions, hobbies, and goals . . . *just like them!*
- Establish a tone of mutual respect for one another that is displayed at all times—this respect must be student to teacher, student to student, and teacher to student. It is important to treat students with respect and expect the same from them.
- Establish rules and standards for behavior in your classroom. You may have them already in mind or allow the students to assist you with the class rules (remember to limit the list to five or six rules). Post them in the room, and send a copy home to parents with a letter of introduction. You may want to send it as a tear-off that parents must sign. I would also have the rules in your class newsletter or as a handout during Open House.
- Choose rules that you and your students can live with.
- Maintain these rules for *everyone* in your room.

BE FAIR AND CONSISTENT

Do not send Johnny out of the room for committing the same infraction that Jane did 20 minutes earlier. Students resent teachers who allow a double standard to exist in the classroom.

- Address undesirable behavior when it first occurs—unchecked misbehavior may result in a greater disruption down the line.
- Establish direct eye contact with the child so he or she perceives the seriousness of what you are saying to him or her.
- Use proximity to physically place yourself near the student (along with a firm look or a soft tap on the desktop) so he or she understands that the behavior is not appropriate.

- Deal with discipline in a calm, low, deliberate manner—
the antithesis of the behavior you are trying to dispel.
- Model desirable behaviors.
- Review with students at the onset of the school year
possible disciplinary actions if the rules are not followed.
- Remain consistent with these rules throughout the
school year.

Strategies 1 through 8 are for your use as the manager of
your classroom without interventions from administrators:

1. *Warning*—Most daily, nonthreatening disturbances
simply require that the teacher stay calm and respectful while
maintaining a firm tone to remind the students that they are
not following a desired behavior—talking to peers, getting
out of their seats without permission, writing on the desk,
passing notes, being inattentive, and so on.

> Most of these behaviors can be addressed through
> a. Verbal reminder
> b. Eye contact
> c. Proximity
> d. Calling student's name with clear instructions on
>   how to rectify the disruptive behavior

2. *Time out or time in*—Teachers usually use the term *time
out*, but it is better to approach this strategy as a time for
students to reflect inwardly, or "time in," about an incident
using a behavior journal (see Strategy 3).

Be careful to align the offense with the time in or out; that
is, a 30-minute time in or out for talking with a friend is not
appropriate. Either can be done in a designated area in your
classroom or with a neighboring teacher. (Make sure that this
arrangement is agreed on beforehand and it is mutual.)

3. *Behavior journal*—Students may be given the opportunity to sit in a designated area in the classroom to complete
a behavior journal. It could require that the student describe
the offense and how he or she could have handled it more
productively. This is generally used when the behavior is not
extremely disruptive.

4. *Withhold privileges or position*—This may include keeping the child in from recess or nutrition (they must still be allowed to use the bathroom) or not being the "jump rope monitor" for that day. I would not recommend keeping the child from a field trip or extracurricular activity, since these are related to instruction, unless there is a serious infraction. I would also recommend having crackers, boxed juices, or another type of snack available for students or making arrangements for the student to stay in the following day after speaking to the parent that evening. This way, the student can pack a snack or lunch that night or morning.

5. *Write a letter of apology*—Write to the person the student offended or send an explanation to the parent.

6. *Call home*—Parents are generally willing to assist the teacher with follow through at home about an inappropriate behavior at school. They cannot assist you, however, if you do not contact them and make them aware that there is a concern.

7. *Note or letter to parent*—If the behavior persists, I would follow up an initial phone call with a letter to further inform the parents of their child's progress. The tone of the letter should be cordial, sincere, and professional. If required by your school, it is important to get the letter approved by an administrator before sending it home. During the call or letter, establish an open invitation for the parents to visit class, return the call, or set aside a time to meet.

8. *Daily or weekly progress report*—If the student is displaying challenges in his or her ability to keep up with classwork or homework, it often helps if the teacher makes note of the assignments in the student's agenda book or sends a weekly progress report home to communicate short-term improvements.

Special Note: It is my experience that students who display habitual disciplinary challenges usually have something else going on in their lives that is adversely affecting their ability to follow the school's codes of conduct. It is at this point that more stringent interventions need to directly and consistently involve the parents, other members of the family, support personnel, or administrators.

Strategies 9 through 12 may be necessary if the behaviors exhibited by a student are repeatedly disruptive or create an unsafe environment for other students. As a classroom manager, you must use sound judgment to determine when it is appropriate to take more serious actions or interventions. It is also essential that you really know your students. Sometimes disruptive behavior is an outward indicator that there are troubling emotions inside the heart and mind of a student.

9. *Conferencing*—If a student's behavior is repeatedly disruptive, then it is time to have a conference. This could include conversations with the

> Adult counselor
>
> Peer counselor
>
> Teacher-parent-student
>
> Teacher-administrator-student
>
> Teacher-administrator-student-parents

10. *In-house suspension*—I have not found any research substantiating that suspensions change behavior. On the contrary, a suspension alienates students, prevents them from attending class and completing assignments, and causes them to fall further behind in their schoolwork. Instead, I think students should stay in school, particularly if the behavior is nonthreatening. This could mean doing community service in a classroom of students at the lower grades or completing a packet of work in another colleague's classroom. Faculty and staff may want to collaboratively develop a list of options for in-house suspensions.

11. *Suspension*—If there is a volatile or dangerous situation, then it is best to remove students from the classroom altogether. It may also be necessary to suspend students from school if it is warranted to resolve a situation.

12. *School police, police, or expulsion*—Each school district has specific criteria for calling the police or expelling a student from the school or school district. Each teacher needs to be very knowledgeable about these infractions and the immediate protocol to skip over Strategies 1 through 11 and go directly to 12. Incidences of arson or weapons or drug possession would fall in this category. In addition, if there is any suspicion of child abuse, a teacher is to contact an administrator, the police, or social services immediately.

Special Note: A combination of the suggested strategies from this list can also be used. For example, a teacher may warn a child and call his or her home. Unfortunately, sending a student to the office is not always an effective disciplinary measure, because the disruptive student may see it as a treat to get out of class. It may be a much more powerful message to the disruptive student (and the entire class) to have the student stay in a designated area in your classroom to complete his or her work. Another noninvasive strategy may be to ask a neighboring teacher to allow the student to stay in his or her classroom. It is important that you offer these same services if your neighbor ever needs to remove a disruptive student. These measures, of course, are for minor infractions that do not necessarily require administrative intervention. Again, make sure the intervention fits the offense. You do not want a student to miss too much instructional time for talking to a friend or eating in class, for example.

In addition, I have not found that assigning students to write standards to be effective, and in many school districts, writing standards is considered a form of corporal punishment. Besides, by the time the student has completed those 100 repetitions, the significance of doing them has diminished without any systemic changes in behavior!

KEY POINTS TO REMEMBER

- If there is a problem, talk to your student one-on-one (the sooner the better).

- Stepping out of the room with the student is helpful. Remember to engage the remaining students in an independent activity, while talking to the student outside.

Often, students who are "bad" in class tend to really be upset about something else unrelated to the classroom, such as a death in the family; a fight with a sibling; not having breakfast that morning; losing a game, friend, or contest; or family or personal problems.

- Inappropriate behavior is a child's way of communicating "Help me!"
- Do not embarrass, criticize, or humiliate children in front of their peers. "Saving face" is much more important to them than being sent out of your classroom.
- Assist students with strategies for opening the lines of communication.
- Teach students problem-solving techniques. Engage them in role playing.
- Listen to both sides of an argument. Be impartial.
- Keep lessons structured. Plan the day with engaging and varied instructional activities planned from bell to bell—there will be less opportunity for students to act up.

I always told my students that if they were having a problem, just tell me. I did not want my students to come into the classroom with an attitude, starting arguments or fighting, or so cranky that everyone had to tiptoe on eggshells around them. Every member of the classroom was an active part of our learning community. We were not a part of the problem, but we could all strive to be a part of the solution.

When students are acting out in class, it is invariably an indication that something else is going on in that child's life. Teachers know that they must not personalize what students do; it really is not about the teacher. It is valuable to remember that children look to the teacher for more than academic development. Teachers take on the role of surrogate parent and provide emotional and moral development as well. A great teacher must look beyond the behavior to the deeper issues going on in the child's life.

It is also important for teachers to clearly explain to students that dealing with personal problems does not justify the disruption of the entire class. Each student plays a vital role toward the success of the entire day by exercising self-control and respect for others.

When I was a classroom teacher, I purposely faced the students' desks in the opposite direction of my desk. In addition, I always placed my desk in the rear of the room and a chair was placed next to my desk. While students were completing their warm-up activity, it was not uncommon for students to come back to my desk and share briefly any situation that they felt might cause them not to do their best work or adversely affect their performance that day. I was amazed at the increased frequency and variety of students who would slip into that chair while I was taking roll! They just needed a few minutes to chat. I found that this brief interlude really diminished the number of behavior problems or outbursts in my class!

Seating arrangements have also proven to be another very successful strategy to offset potential interruptions. Avoid clustering all boys, all girls, or all same-race students. Instead, distribute the boys, girls, and races evenly throughout the classroom by using your well-planned seating chart. This also encourages students to develop the ability to work efficiently with a variety of people, not just their friends. After all, isn't that what adults are expected to do in the workplace?

LEADERSHIP OPPORTUNITIES DIMINISH DISCIPLINARY CHALLENGES

Leadership opportunities among students in your classroom can enhance academic success, self-esteem, cooperation, and communication skills. Ultimately, you will begin to see the implementation of student leadership diminish many disciplinary problems in the classroom.

School or classroom rules may encourage students to be docile, unresponsive, and uncommunicative. Schools teach students that if they are quiet, then they are considered model students, while the rambunctious types are labeled as troublemakers.

A great teacher, however, knows that he or she must allow students the opportunity to ask questions, challenge concepts, explore controversial issues, and even intellectually disagree with the educator's opinion. Great teachers view themselves as facilitators and instructional coaches.

They know that constant use of fill-in-the-blank dittos and handouts, lectures, copying sentences, standards, and other potentially ho-hum busywork does not develop leadership skills or higher levels of critical thinking. Busywork may cause some students to display the very disruptive behaviors that teachers were really trying to avoid. When students are bored and unchallenged, they create their own fun. A teacher's keen intuition about the students' learning styles necessitates that the teacher continuously create instructional activities that will ensure ongoing student engagement.

Here are some examples of roles, tasks, and activities that can enhance student leadership skills and develop character and that will reinforce such attributes as self-control, self-esteem, critical thinking, problem solving, and accountability:

- Monitor
- Line leader
- Group leader
- Peer tutor
- Student council member
- Class officer
- Teacher for the day
- Student-directed lessons
- Cooperative and collaborative learning

Other leadership-enhancing activities you can try may include allowing your students to:

- Write the current date at a designated location on the white or bulletin board
- Bring the class to order in the morning
- Return graded papers
- Lead small-group activities
- Tutor other students
- Read the homeroom bulletin
- Pick up or deliver materials to the office
- Erase the board at the end of the day
- Write the agenda on the board in the morning
- Organize and plan classroom events or field trips
- Distribute textbooks
- Lead oral recitations (Pledge of Allegiance, morning poetry, affirmations)
- Collect homework
- Greet visitors to the class
- Assist with beautification of the room
- Others?

True Story

A veteran teacher who was new to one of my schools shared her concern with site administrators that she was having great difficulty with the "discipline problems" in her class. It seemed that no matter how hard she tried, the majority of the students were not able to complete their assignments in a timely fashion. They were also disrespectful and unruly. She was sure that she had inherited every bad student in the school and was sent to the bowels of the campus in a basement space that was converted into a classroom. As the secondary instructional adviser, I was asked to visit the teacher's class to provide some possible suggestions to resolve these ongoing challenges.

My initial impression was that the room was far too small, with a class of students that was too large! In addition, there was no teaching assistant or service worker to help. The high school students in that classroom had learned very quickly to manipulate both situations to their advantage. Students would repeatedly raise their hands to ask the teacher for clarification on a specific aspect of the lesson. The students also kept the teacher busy getting them the necessary books, paper, and pens they needed to complete the assignment. The students would knowingly wink at one another as they sent the teacher on an obstacle course through a maze of desks and students, and a barrage of trite questions. The students could play this "game" because the teacher did not fully explain the lesson or distribute the necessary materials at the onset. This gave the students a mechanism by which to keep her busy, allowing them to chat when her back was turned to assist other students.

During a post-conference with the teacher, I described what I observed during my hour in the classroom. I suggested that she spend more time at the onset explaining the lesson, providing a rubric (scoring guide, criteria chart), entertaining questions, and possibly showing student work samples as "anchor" papers. She might also enhance understanding by asking students to repeat the directions or explain in their own words the important aspects of the task. I also suggested that she develop procedures for assigning student monitors to pass out the books and other resource materials. This would allow her to maintain a visible position in the classroom to monitor all of the activity among her students. It worked! She contacted me weeks later indicating that the persistent discipline problems had subsided and the students "weren't so bad after all."

Extra Seasoning

A Win-Win Outcome

It is clear that classroom management and student discipline are totally interconnected. On one hand, classroom management is not something that "just happens." It must be strategically planned prior to the beginning of the school year.

All students deserve to have an organized classroom with rules and procedures that are fair, clear, and consistent. On the other hand, most discipline problems can be avoided when there is an efficient classroom management system in place beginning the first day of school. This system also proves to have a direct impact on students' academic achievement. That's what I call a win-win outcome!

Savory Morsel

Many administrators are looking for teachers who can manage classrooms effectively, because they know that good learning can only take place when order and discipline are the rules rather than the exception.

—Rebecca Lynn Wilke (2003, p. 60)

Reflection Menu

- How do you set guidelines for student behavior at the onset of the school year?
- What measures do you use to ensure that standards for student behavior are upheld?
- How do you effectively balance rules, rewards, and consequences?

If You Like This Ingredient, You'll Also Like . . .

Ingredient 3

Ingredient 5

Organizational Skills

Celebrating Successful Recipes

During my tenure as a classroom teacher, I required all of my students to maintain a three-ring notebook with five sections separated by dividers. You may have another type of notebook that best suits the manner in which you want your students to organize their work. The important point here is that students of all ages need to learn to be responsible for their own assignments. These organizational skills can transfer to the organization of assignments in other classes, extracurricular activities, and even their belongings and responsibilities at home.

PURCHASING NOTEBOOK MATERIALS

Be sensitive here, teachers. If you have students who genuinely cannot afford a notebook or dividers, you may opt to give them helpful tasks in class to earn "class bucks," then provide them with the opportunity to "purchase" the supplies from you.

I have always experienced a positive response from parents who are more than willing to purchase materials that will facilitate instruction. They understand the value of having their children organize their work, and it certainly facilitates the parents' ability to support the completion of homework and projects required beyond the school day. In addition, students can give an account of their work during parent conferences and Student-Led Conferences, which further validates the grades or marks students eventually receive on their report cards.

It is highly recommended that you send a note home briefly explaining the purpose for needing any extra school supplies and how they tie into preparing the students for academic success.

It is important to show consideration for the parents' time by allowing the students several days to get all of the necessary supplies. I usually give my students a week (including a weekend). This gives working parents an opportunity to purchase these items over the weekend, instead of shopping at the end of a long workday. There may be some students who will wait until 8 o'clock at night to tell their parents about the notebook and dividers. (I'm sure this does not fit the description of any of your students.)

Example in English

Dear Parents,

In an effort to reinforce with my students the importance of neatness, organization, and accountability, I have asked each student to bring a three-ring notebook, five dividers, standard lined paper, and at least two black or blue ink pens. The students will have five distinct sections in their notebooks.

Thank you in advance for your cooperation as I endeavor to uphold academic excellence in my classroom.

Sincerely,

Mrs. Moultrie Turner

Example in Spanish

Estimados Padres,

Yo le he pedido a cada estudiante que traiga reforzar con mis estudiantes la importancia de limpieza, organización, y responsabilidad, en un esfuerzo un tres-ring cuaderno, cinco divisores, el papel lineado normal, y por lo menos dos plumas de tinta negras o azules para clasificar. Los estudiantes tendrán cinco secciones distintas en sus cuadernos.

Gracias por adelantado por su cooperación cuando yo el esfuerzo por levantar la excelencia académica en mi aula.

Atentamente,

Anita Moultrie Turner

Special Note: If the office staff can distribute your class roster before the year begins, this would provide ample time to mail a letter of introduction to parents during the summer.

The students and I walk through the organization of their notebook together by the second week of school. I encourage students to keep their notebook in some type of folder (or I may provide a manila folder for students who need one) while we are allowing all of the students the week to secure the required supplies. In fact, most of the first week of school is spent on team-building activities; therefore, the amount of paperwork is minimal.

After sufficient time has been provided, I designate a day in class to assist students with the organization of their notebooks according to my guidelines. This process takes approximately 30 minutes during class time. Although they are provided with a rubric, I still find it helpful to take some time from the lesson to organize the notebook together.

It is important to note here that I initially provide the guidelines for the structure of the notebook so that everyone is uniform, and this allows me to easily and efficiently correct their notebooks in a short amount of time. Eventually, you may allow students the flexibility to decide on the organization of their own notebook in a way that makes sense for them. Without question, it is of equal value that students are allowed autonomy and independence to make decisions that will promote their own academic development.

Generally, any student enrolling after this initial day of walking through the notebook will receive instructions from a reliable student who has clearly shown his or her own expertise in keeping an organized notebook.

When the notebook is opened, the first page is the title page. I can immediately identify who is the owner of the notebook, the period, and subject. This page can also be a lifesaver if the students happen to leave their notebooks in another class!

Honestly, I've had notebooks returned from other rooms, the lunch area, and the library because the students had their names written on the title page (see Figure 8.1).

The second page is the table of contents (see Figure 8.2). No page numbers are assigned. I do ask, however, that everyone's notebook is arranged in the same order. (This helps me to correct them faster and note if the students are able to follow a specific order.) The key to success here is that your students are demonstrating consistency in their organizational skills.

Special Note:

- You may choose your own notebook order, categories, and sections.
- Sections are organized into five categories—classwork, homework, tests and quizzes, and warm-ups and journals.
- Consistency among every student allows you to correct the notebooks expeditiously.

(I did not take the students' notebooks home. They were corrected during dispatch time or during a quiet activity in class.)

The third page is the assignment sheet (see Figure 8.3). Each time the students received an assignment, the title of the

Figure 8.1 Notebook Title Page

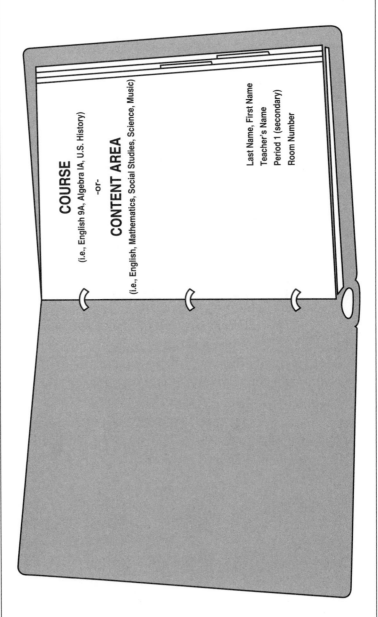

COURSE

(i.e., English 9A, Algebra IA, U.S. History)

-or-

CONTENT AREA

(i.e., English, Mathematics, Social Studies, Science, Music)

Last Name, First Name
Teacher's Name
Period 1 (secondary)
Room Number

Figure 8.2 Table of Contents Page

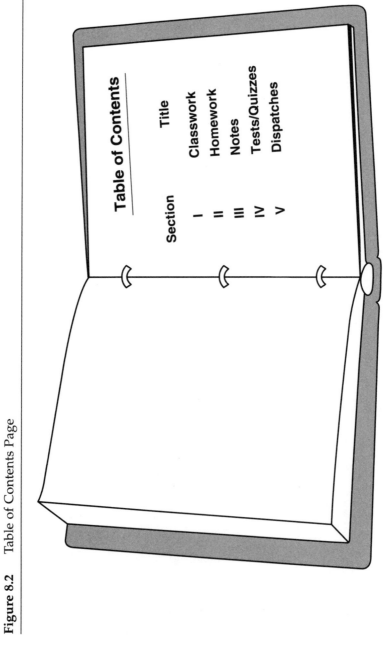

Figure 8.3   Assignment Sheet Page

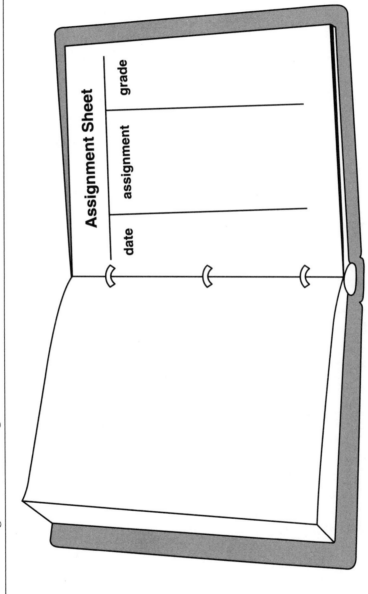

assignment was placed on this sheet. Once the assignment was corrected and returned, the grade was placed on the assignment sheet as well. A larger version was written on the chalkboard or posted on the bulletin board.

This served five distinct purposes:

1. Students know exactly what they are expected to do.

2. Students have an immediate record of their progress.

3. Absentees know the assignments they need to make up.

4. Students know which assignments will be used to determine their report card grade.

5. Students have a running record of their assignments, grades, and the exact dates the work was assigned to the class.

Section 1—Classwork

Any lessons, assignments, or projects that are completed in class are placed in this section. All work must be organized in date order. (I gave the students the choice of least recent to most recent or vice versa.)

Section 2—Homework

Any lessons, assignments, or projects that were completed at home were placed in this section. All work must be organized in date order.

Section 3—Notes

Students of all ages can learn how to take effective notes from directed lessons, oral discussions, board work, overhead transparencies, sustained silent reading cooperative learning groups, or any other instructional activity. Taking notes is an important lifelong skill that will facilitate students' success at all levels of education, including colleges and universities. All work must be organized in date order.

Often I would put my personal notes on the overhead projector after my students had completed their own notes during a directed lesson. This provided the opportunity for students to compare their note taking with mine. I wanted the students to ask themselves such questions as the following:

- Did I get all of the pertinent information while I was taking notes?
- Were my notes clearly written to be a useful study tool in preparation for a test or follow-up activity?
- Is there a more concise way to document important information?
- In what ways can I improve my ability to take effective notes?

As the teacher, it is important that you purposely create situations that afford students the opportunity to practice taking notes. They will continually get better as they practice this vital skill.

Section 4—Tests and Quizzes

Any test or quiz is placed in this section. All work must be organized in date order.

Section 5—Journal/Diary/Dispatch/Warm-Up

Most students do not spend enough time writing. Either I required them to write one full page each day on any topic in a personal diary format, or I had them write one full page each day on a given topic, famous quote, dilemma, or proverb. (See journal assignments in Ingredient 6.)

S-t-r-e-t-c-h your students not to just write within their comfort zone . . . if you give them the option of how much to write, you may only get a few sentences. Depending on the academic level of your class, you may start with asking them to write a half a page, then three quarters of a page, then a full page. You will find that most students who begin the year laboring through the writing of one paragraph eventually write a full page or more with greater ease, skill, and proficiency.

This activity is completed in approximately the first 10 minutes of the day or class period . . . every day! As stated previously, this gives students a chance to settle down, get focused, and develop their writing skills—all at the same time!

In fact, to my great pleasure, my students really looked forward to having this time to pen their thoughts. They were actually disappointed if there were some unforeseen reason why they would not have time to write in class (i.e., shortened day, guest speaker).

Be careful when you have the students complete a diary instead of writing on a designated topic. Set parameters for what is appropriate and inappropriate in this assignment. It is important that students know that their privacy would be respected. Many times, my students would ask me to read a particular entry because they wanted to share a concern or issue. This allowed me to connect with my students and open a line of communication to discuss things that were really bothering them.

I did admonish students, however, to recognize the assignment as a school activity. Since it was kept in their notebooks, they were not to write on extremely private or sensitive issues. I was concerned that if their notebooks became misplaced on campus, other students might have access to this personal information. Eventually, I kept composition books in a locked cabinet while students worked on writing in a diary to protect their confidentiality. The other journal and dispatch entries remained in their three-ring notebooks.

Dispatches and journals were submitted and corrected at the end of the week, and students received a grade for writing five full pages because I was asking them to compose—to just write (often called a *quickwrite*). During other portions of instructional time, we would look more closely at their specific composition and grammatical skills.

There should be a folder on the teacher's desk or a designated table documenting each journal or dispatch entry. This made it very accessible for absentees to retrieve the folder, write the topic, and then turn in a completed journal for the week. The folder also diminished any potential excuses students might use for not completing their work. (This is one reason why I did not require the journal to be submitted until the end of the week.) I also encouraged students to find a "buddy" they could call to get the entry title or subject and already have it completed when they returned to school after an absence.

To ease your workload, I would have a responsible student post the entry each day in the dispatch or journal folder (see Figure 8.4).

Special Note: Elementary students (fourth–sixth grade) are mature enough to keep their work organized in some kind of notebook. Younger students (kindergarten–third grade) should keep at least a classwork and homework folder in date order, and the work can go home at the end of the week.

You know your students better than I do (of course), so just be sure to keep your criteria for the notebook (or anything else) clear, precise, and detailed for them! If your second graders, for example, can organize and maintain a multisectioned notebook, then I would certainly suggest that you encourage them to step up to the challenge!

It is important to note that this writing practice during the warm-up portion of your class time should not take the place of the vital need to engage your students in targeted instruction to develop their writing skills.

A completed notebook (see Figure 8.5) will facilitate much more organized young people in your classroom!

Figure 8.4 Dispatch Folder

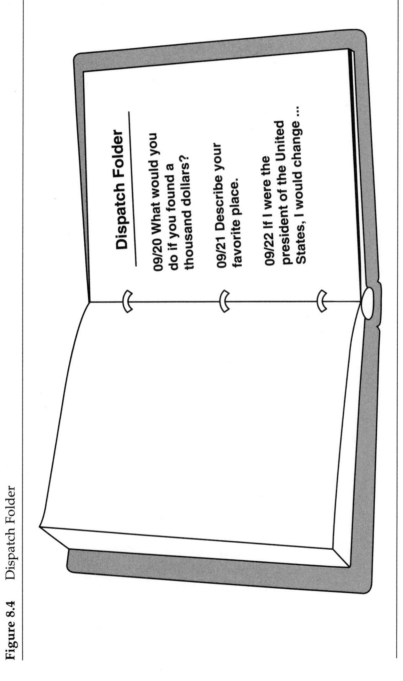

Dispatch Folder

09/20 What would you do if you found a thousand dollars?

09/21 Describe your favorite place.

09/22 If I were the president of the United States, I would change ...

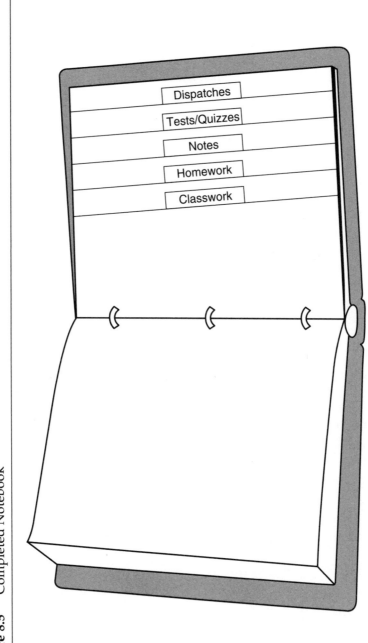

Figure 8.5 Completed Notebook

True Story

There was an incident in which one of my students left her notebook on the city bus, and it eventually found its way back to school! One of my very bright and talented students was studying for a test we were having that day. She took out her notebook and began to study her notes as she rode to school. When my student realized that she was getting close to her designated stop, she set the notebook down on the seat to check on some other items in her backpack. Unfortunately, in her rush to exit the bus, she forgot to pick up the notebook from the seat. My student frantically rushed into the classroom to explain her dilemma. She knew that her notebook had every assignment the students had done in class since the beginning of the school year. I reminded her that her name was in the front of the notebook, and there was a strong possibility that it could somehow find its way back to her. Sure enough, another passenger found the notebook and gave it to the bus driver. The next morning, he returned it to his young and very grateful passenger!

Extra Seasoning

Notebooks are a great way to provide ongoing assistance to students to take ownership for their own learning and the organizing of that learning. I have seen countless desks, backpacks, and notebooks that are in total disarray. Students have no idea what work they have completed, submitted, or received with a score or grade. Organized notebooks provide "checks and balances" to your grade book, and students have a clear understanding of how they are progressing in your class.

Of course, as adults, we must organize appointments, bill payment, family life, and work. As frustrating as it might seem to students, being able to organize oneself will have a lifelong impact on their academic and career experiences. In fact, this is consistently confirmed as I work with university professors who explain that organization is one factor that contributes to the overall success of college students.

SAVORY MORSEL

Success on any major scale requires you to accept responsibility . . . in the final analysis, the one quality that all successful people have . . . is the ability to take on responsibility.

—Michael Korda (as cited in
benShea, 2002, p. 137)

REFLECTION MENU

- Why is it important for your students to learn organizational skills?
- How does your classroom dynamic reflect your own organizational skills?
- What other opportunities can you create in your class to teach organizational skills?

IF YOU LIKE THIS INGREDIENT, YOU'LL ALSO LIKE . . .

Ingredient 6

Ingredient 9

Real-Life Skills

Cuisine for Life Beyond the Classroom

INTEGRATING REAL-LIFE SKILLS
ACROSS THE CURRICULUM

It is vital for students to understand that the skills they learn in school should be transferred to the actual skills they will need to be a successful, healthy, and prosperous adult. It would be a wise decision on the part of your faculty, grade level, or department to collaboratively create real-life skills that can be integrated into lessons, exercises, or activities during instructional time in each content area.

Most school districts have grade-level meetings or common planning time during which collaboration is encouraged and appropriated during school hours. In addition, teachers may collectively agree to set aside a part of their summer or off-track time to prepare units that infuse real-life skills that culminate in an interdisciplinary project as they map out the curriculum for the following year.

Elementary teachers generally have the same children or a shared number of students to work with each day. For this reason, it is very do-able to integrate interesting real-life activities into the students' instructional day. If the students are reading a story, for example, they can create an advertisement, write a friendly letter to a character, design an invitation for one character to send to another, or send a character the directions to a major event taking place in the story.

Real-life skills can also be integrated across the curriculum. Let's consider the study of missions traditionally studied in the fourth grade. As an art project, students must use mathematical skills to create the appropriate measurements to build a model of a mission. Science can be integrated by using Internet sources to determine the elements used in the building materials of these amazing structures that have stood for so many years. During the social studies unit, you can impress upon young people that societal, political, educational, and economic issues are influenced by the media. Creating a student-based newspaper could include articles written by students describing various missions and distributed to other fourth-grade classes or the entire school. Students could design invitations to other classes to view models of missions they may have on display in the classroom. The students may also create a cookbook with popular foods eaten during that time, culminating with a taste-testing feast by the participants. It would also be fun for students to write a letter to their parents sharing what they have learned during this unit and inviting them to take part in the activities as well. These suggestions are intended to show the reader that real-life skills can easily be integrated into the curriculum with a little creativity and ingenuity. Trust me, your class will become a big hit for the students and their families!

Secondary teachers generally have a larger number of students during the course of a day, and their content areas are departmentalized. Even with these challenges, a secondary classroom teacher in any content area can still infuse real-life activities into a lesson, homework, or extended learning activity. It is also exciting to team with other colleagues from various departments to create opportunities for interdisciplinary teaching while embedding real-life skills. In addition, many high schools currently require students to complete a lifeskills course as a prerequisite for attaining their diploma.

Secondary students may have a skewed perception of the relevance and applicability of their education. It has been my experience that many secondary students feel as though Period 1 science has nothing to do with Period 2 English, which has nothing to do with Period 3 social studies, and so on . . . you get the picture. It is not until students truly make a connection between what happens each period in every content area that they will really move to a more mature and comprehensive level in their education. Teachers are really the best facilitators to make that connection happen for secondary students.

This is especially true if teachers share a core of students. The English teacher, for example, may read *Romeo and Juliet* and have the students do the wedding planning for the lovers or create the invitations for the masquerade party. Furthermore, the math teacher may team with the English teacher and have the students create timelines, graphs, charts, or even an imaginary budget for the heart-struck lovers to live independently from their parents. The social studies teacher may have the students devise a route of escape using an imaginary map with a legend and directions to their hiding place or study the customs, religions, and traditions of the Shakespearean era. Think out of the box! It is these creative, engaging, and hands-on activities that help students make lifelong connections between the instructional program and their own lives!

Great educators understand that real-life skills are an essential part of students' instruction because they are necessary for them to be successful in this fast-paced and dynamic society as adults. Students do not, however, automatically acquire these skills by attending school every day. It is up to teachers to deliberately integrate these real-life skills into the students' daily instructional activities.

Real-life skills can also be acquired through leadership opportunities such as a service worker in the library, student store, office, or lunch or snack line. The students can organize fundraisers, school festivals, dances, concerts, or bake sales. Since community service hours are generally a graduation requirement for high school students, the ninth through twelfth graders can plan, organize, or facilitate an activity at a local church, retirement home, child care center, or homeless shelter. The high school students can even team with the local elementary or middle schools to plan a community event such as a food bank for the homeless, sports program, afterschool tutoring, or a talent show! Supervising adults should require that students be directly responsible for the planning, design, and implementation of the event to ensure that they learn those vital real-life skills firsthand.

Parent Involvement

I would also suggest that your grade level or departmental team devise a list of ways that parents can reinforce these real-life skills at home and distribute them during Open House or Back to School night. There are many real-life skills inherent in the seemingly mundane chores that we as adults just do because they are part of our routine. These daily responsibilities can become "teachable moments" for functional skills that are life's lessons for children. Using real-life skills is easy to do when children accompany their parents to the grocery store, bank, post office, airport, shopping mall, restaurants, or cleaners. Check resource books, textbooks, bookstores, or your local libraries for materials that can be used in the classroom or shared with parents for use at home.

There are many important reasons to include real-life skills into your lesson planning:

a. Some standardized state tests include questions related to "functional reading," which may include such tasks as reading washing instructions on the label of a garment, following directions to a recipe, reading a chart, entering a contest from a cereal box, reading a utility bill, or ordering from a menu.

b. Students will learn to become more independent as young adults.

c. In the event of an emergency or critical situation, students will respond appropriately or may potentially save their own lives or those of others.

d. Students may become better stewards of their own money, time, relationships, and resources.

It is not uncommon for some students graduating from high school to experience frustration in going away to college and living on their own. This may happen due to academic challenges, but young people may find it an even greater challenge to survive the everyday skills necessary to make it on their own. This gives the adults in their lives an even greater challenge and responsibility to make sure that young people are competent in the effective execution of real-life skills.

The following is a sample list of important real-life (functional) skills:

- Using applications
- Banking
- Budgeting
- Writing and reading classified ads
- Completing a ballot
- Having computer literacy
- Using credit cards
- Reading department store catalogs
- Figuring sales tax
- Following and giving directions
- Writing form letters
- Reading how-to's
- Interviewing
- Writing invitations

- Making appointments
- Making reservations
- Communicating orally
- Going to the post office
- Reading labels
- Reading maps
- Writing resumes
- Settling disputes
- Shopping (use of coupons, comparative/bargain shopping)
- Reading signs
- Using telephone books and directories
- Using telephone courtesies
- Reading utility bills

Can you add to this list?

True Story

One of the novels on the English department's core list was *Jubilee* by Margaret Walker. This story had its foundations from an extensive interview Walker had with her grandmother. As an enrichment activity, I asked students to interview a senior citizen of at least 65 years or older. Some of the students had close ties to their own grandparents, and others had to go to retirement homes. Next, I had the students interview them using questions that were devised during class. The students were also required to ask the seniors for their favorite recipe and the story associated with this dish. Ultimately, we created a cookbook that included personal stories, visuals, and outstanding recipes. Finally, we created personalized note cards and invited administrators, staff, and parents to a fabulously delicious potluck featuring many of these great dishes. Most of the dishes were cooked by the students themselves!

Can you identify all of the real-life skills featured in these enrichment activities?

Extra Seasoning

Regardless of your grade level or content area, you must understand that students will leave you a year older and, hopefully, a year wiser. If you view students with their future in mind, it will be critical to empower them with skills that will support their future responsibilities and goals. As great teachers, you want to have a far-reaching and poignant impact on the lives of your students in terms of their proficiency in your content area and their ability to apply these skills effectively in professional, educational, or real-life situations as adults. It is like casting feathers to the wind and never knowing where they will ultimately end. You cannot predict the future of your students, but you can do everything possible in the school year to develop the skills necessary for their ultimate success. I did not see myself as an English teacher, but as a teacher who taught English to *students*. Can we please continue to factor students into the equation? This gives more credence to the true meaning of a "student-centered" instructional program.

Savory Morsel

The mere imparting of information is not education.

Above all things, the effort must result in making

A man think and do for himself.

—Carter G. Woodson, 1933
(as cited in Bell, 1995, p. 109)

Reflection Menu

- Can you list all of the real-life skills you need daily to live on your own? your students need?

- How do you reinforce real-life skills in your classroom?
- Consider strategies to encourage parents to use these skills with their children at home.

IF YOU LIKE THIS INGREDIENT, YOU'LL ALSO LIKE . . .

Ingredient 2

Ingredient 4

INGREDIENT 10

The Whole Dinner

Collaboration and Equity

To really dish up a savory and nutritious meal, there are many factors a great chef must consider. Of course, before any pot or pan is even placed on the stove, ingredients, seasonings, and garnishments must be carefully planned in preparation for creating a perfect meal to please everyone's palate. The same is true for a great classroom teacher, who considers the essential ingredients of an academic feast as well as his or her role in supporting the overall educational "menu" of the entire school.

PROMOTING STAFF INVOLVEMENT

Many schools have processes such as Critical Friends, Collaborative Friends, and interdisciplinary teams to facilitate an ongoing dialogue among colleagues. They may involve team building, weekly or monthly meetings, lesson planning, observations in one another's classrooms, and analyses of authentic student work samples. These are concepts that promote adult professional development and that directly link to student learning through collegial relationships, supporting reflective practice, and rethinking leadership. They are vital for the development of shared norms, shared resources, and ideas, as well as giving one another feedback on practices and effectively impacting the school's organization and culture.

A great teacher understands the importance of working in collaboration with other faculty members. To really enact positive schoolwide changes requires the concerted efforts of each administrator, teacher, and classified staff. The most successful schools have administrators and staff members who understand that teachers cannot work in a vacuum. Despite the fact that a classroom teacher is isolated with his or her students for most of the day, it is vital to come from the classroom and sit down with colleagues to discuss issues, concerns, lessons, or projects that will benefit the entire student body.

As part of powerful learning communities, teachers can have a direct impact on academic rigor and the cultural, intellectual, emotional, and social development of their students. In the book *On Common Ground: The Power of Professional Learning Communities*, Mike Schmoker (2005) emphatically explains:

> If there is anything that the research community agrees on, it is this: The right kind of continuous, structured teacher collaboration improves the quality of teaching and pays big, often immediate, dividends in student learning and professional morale in virtually any setting. (p. xii)

As the principal of the Accelerated Charter School, I believed so much in the power of the classroom teacher to effect a positive school culture, motivate students to excellence, critically view their own practices, and allow other colleagues to be a sounding board for the creation and implementation of best practices that I created a bell schedule that allowed for daily opportunities for teachers to come together. Among other stakeholders, it is also the great teacher who has his or her heart, soul, and sensibilities on the pulse of the school's overall well-being. I always told my staff that as the principal, I needed their frequent, honest, and thoughtful input because I was smarter with them than I was by myself!

We believed that our students were totally worth our continuous and highly visible commitment and nurturing. Without compromise, the staff collaboratively agreed on the philosophy that it was not OK for our students to fail. Now, what were we going to do about it? This kind of work did not come without a price: time, effort, prayer and meditation, praise, and accountable talk. These conversations were frequent and ongoing, absolutely not haphazard. None of us wanted to experience failure: myself, the teachers, or the students we endeavored to educate! It was this kind of ongoing collaboration that created a tremendous academic, social, and emotional change on the precious lives of children attending a school located in the heart of an urban community.

It is with great disappointment that students at varying socioeconomic, racial, or religious levels experience failures in school. Unfortunately, disobedience, disrespect, and despair may become the byproduct of these continuous negative experiences. To minimize the hurt of these failures, students may adopt a belief that "if I don't try, then it won't matter if I fail."

Whether we work in urban, rural, or suburban school districts, it is essential that we continuously revitalize our clientele. The issues plaguing our students may be different, but the academic, social, and emotional outcomes may be the same. It is imperative that we give them frequent entrees of hope, accomplishment, success, and well-being. It is a worthy investment for every teacher to cultivate the talents and skills of every student. After all, the very child that we inspire may eventually make a powerful and tremendous contribution to society in years to come.

I highly recommend that you read *Gifted Hands* (1990) and *Think Big* (1992) by Dr. Ben S. Carson. He was tragically labeled the "class dummy" as a fifth-grade student. Although his mother was not a good reader herself, she insisted that Dr. Carson and his brother read two library books each week and complete a written book report in an effort to thwart their history of failing grades. Fortunately, he soon realized that he was not stupid and within weeks amazed his science teacher and classmates with his newfound knowledge and began a steady progression to the top of his class. This same underachieving African American boy experienced a tremendous turnaround and eventually grew up to be the first neurosurgeon to separate Siamese twins conjoined at the brain! At age 32, he became the director of pediatric neurosurgery at the prestigious Johns Hopkins medical center in Baltimore. This is just one example of the power of an education and people who believe in the abilities of every child to really make a difference in their lives. I encourage you to keep a journal, memory book, diary, or notebook of your own examples of triumphs that were made as you positively influence the lives of your students.

Collaboration can also include taking advantage of opportunities to get involved in the life of the school. I would encourage each educator to become a teacher-leader, along with those who are energetic, assertive, and collaborative, with a focus or project that will promote student achievement. This can be accomplished through faculty meetings, common planning time, departmental or grade-level meetings . . . the sky's the limit! It is absolutely incredible the number of goals that can be successfully accomplished when teachers roll up their sleeves and team together to make them happen!

It is vital to the success of any school to mobilize the energy, talents, and expertise of a group of colleagues who have the same goals and are willing to work together toward some viable strategies that will positively affect the morale, culture, and instructional program of the school. Generally, schools have monies in the budget to allow teachers opportunities for professional development, which could include paid time to meet after school, on Saturdays, during the school day with substitutes, or during off-track time for year-round schools. Take advantage of your veteran teachers, mentor teachers, national board certified teachers, master teachers, department and grade-level chairs, and exemplary teachers, who can share their recognized skills with the entire staff.

I encourage you to align your best practices with the teaching standards established in your state. The California Standards for the Teaching Profession include the following:

Standard One: Engaging and Supporting All Students
                   in Learning

Standard Two: Creating and Maintaining Effective
                   Environments for Student Learning

Standard Three: Understanding and Organizing Subject
                   Matter for Student Learning

Standard Four: Planning Instruction and Designing
                   Learning Experiences for All Students

Standard Five: Assessing Student Learning

Standard Six: Developing as a Professional Educator

Currently, many secondary schools have been implementing small learning communities that generally include a group of 300 to 400 students who have their own administrator, instructional specialist, dean, or counselor, as well as designated teachers. In addition, there are specific goals that all stakeholders understand and plan for using a variety of strategies to address the personal and academic needs of the students through peer observation, self-evaluation, reflective discourse, and ongoing collaboration. This brings to reality the "village raising children" concept on a school campus. Although they are still in the infancy stage in many school districts, small learning communities have proven to impact the academic performance, attendance, standardized test results, and graduation rates for students.

As you plan for success, it is also essential to design programs so that a wide variety of students on your campus will have equal access. It would be unfair to create a great program or activity and limit it to an elite few. It may be more appropriate to identify target student populations for afterschool clubs or organizations celebrating their language, culture, beliefs, values, or lifestyle choices. It can also include the involvement of students through tutoring, sustained silent reading, advisory, book club, decathlon, Saturday school, or study hall. As much as possible, create educational opportunities for every student on your campus.

PROMOTING PARENTAL INVOLVEMENT

It is essential in any great school that the staff involves parents in the planning, establishment, or sustaining of a viable activity or program. On one hand, they are important in a practical manner because they pay for uniforms, dues, instruments, or equipment for the students to participate in the club, team, or organization available at school. Parents must also invest the time, energy, and money to get their children to and from a particular event, rehearsal, or meeting. Parents can also share their expertise by visiting classrooms, participating in school events, volunteering in various events or activities, and maintaining an active role in the lives of their children. Schoolwide and classroom newsletters, homework hotlines, or Web site information can also offer parents suggestions and tips for assisting in their children's academic development.

PROMOTING STUDENT INVOLVEMENT

Collaboration should also include educators honoring students' voices to determine how students feel the school can improve or how to involve more students in the life of the school. More important, they need to agree on ways to actively engage in the implementation of these great programs or events. This could be accomplished through student council, monthly assemblies, advisory, a student section of the daily school bulletin, or a suggestion box in each classroom or office. Students need to believe that staff validate their words, feelings, and interests by listening to their suggestions and putting those that are agreed on into action.

Staff and students need to also devise some strategies to celebrate students' successes, such as student of the month, academic or attendance awards, invitational assemblies or dances, posters, T-shirts, plaques, trophies, banners, bumper stickers, a school paper, and anything else that will encourage students to do their very best. Brainstorm!

It is wonderful to see the entire family sit down to a scrumptious meal during the holidays or special events. The same is true for members of a faculty, staff, and student body. It really takes everyone working together on a school campus to ignite a sense of hope, opportunity, and destiny. The whole dinner is now being served . . . come join us!

True Story

I had the pleasure of being an instructional coach to a very unique elementary school. The principal had a heart of gold, and there was nothing she wouldn't do to support her teachers and students. They knew unequivocally that she loved them all. She believed that her staff was like a second family. They celebrated births, weddings, anniversaries, graduations, birthdays, and the like. It was amazing to me that each time a new teacher was hired to work at this particular school, teachers would meet the new hire on a Saturday and clean his or her room, unload boxes, set up bulletin boards, and do anything else the teacher needed. By the time the teacher started working, the entire room was set up and ready to go. This was true of every aspect of this school, whether that meant raising test scores, self-esteem, attendance, learning environments, community spirit, or academic performance!

Extra Seasoning

Once the ingredients have been identified, it really takes the collaboration of the entire staff to engage in thoughtful dialogue to determine the proportions that will create the best "balanced meal" to ensure a well-nourished faculty and student body. Realistically, every educator is not going to possess every ingredient, but each does possess a measure of talent or skill that supports the vision of the school. It then becomes the responsibility of each faculty member to share his or her areas of strength with one another. The belief that it takes a whole village to raise a child necessitates an open-door policy so that teachers can share their best strategies and techniques with one another.

SAVORY MORSEL

Highly effective teachers possess the moral, intellectual, and social skills to use their leadership for good in the lives of students, parents, and colleagues.

—Elaine K. McEwan (2002, p. 43)

REFLECTION MENU

- Describe the school culture on your campus. Are you actively involved in supporting the academic, social, or community programs at your school?
- Do you have a homework hotline or newsletters accessible for parents to encourage their involvement at the school? in more than one language (when appropriate)?
- Are you knowledgeable about the standards for the teaching profession in your state? How closely are your practices aligned to these standards?

IF YOU LIKE THIS INGREDIENT, YOU'LL ALSO LIKE . . .

Ingredient 3

Ingredient 6

INGREDIENT 11

Welcome to the Table

Now that you have made all of the necessary preparations for the "big feast," it is time to welcome your students to the table. As you can see, there are so many preparations that need to be considered to ensure the flavorful success of your instructional program. It is not enough to attain your teaching credential or to know your content area well. Every ingredient in this book, if measured out with careful considerations, can lead to a rigorous, challenging, and relevant learning environment leading to your students' academic achievement.

FIXINGS FOR A GREAT TEACHER

I want you to see yourself as a great teacher, an exceptional teacher, a powerful teacher who will be remembered by students for many years after they have left your classroom.

Who is this great teacher?

Who is this great teacher who is powerful, insightful, and influential?

Who is this great teacher who encourages students to strive for greatness in their own lives?

A great teacher is mindful of the ingredients described in this text. He or she knows that the execution of a lesson is more than requiring students to read a chapter from a book and answer questions from a handout or assigning the even-numbered problems in a math workbook. Rather, a great teacher has the ability to present a delectable assortment of standards-based activities or lessons that will satisfy even the most finicky intellectual, emotional, and social appetite.

As a classroom teacher, you have the tremendous privilege to positively impact the lives of children. Teaching is a noble, honorable, and challenging profession that affects children, their parents, and their communities. The greatest and most powerful people in our world sat in a teacher's classroom. What an awesome concept!

In future writings, I will take a closer look at additional ingredients for powerful teaching and learning. I will celebrate the tremendous strides of great teachers, schools, and districts as well as examine the research and its applicability to the continued success in your own classroom.

I look forward to our next dinner engagement!

True Story

Colleagues have always asked me to explain the key to my success as a classroom teacher. Despite some challenging experiences and students over the years, I have still managed to excel in my profession. I hold to some very simple beliefs about my work: (a) Teaching is a calling. To make a profound impact, I must embrace that this is about teaching content, but more so about touching the lives of others; (b) I want to be more than an average teacher . . . a good teacher . . . I want to be a *great* teacher; (c) I want to see the potential in every student who crosses the threshold of my classroom; and (d) finally, at the end of the day, I want to proudly say that I strove to do my absolute best!

Extra Seasoning

The impact of our influence on students may not always be evident while they are in our classrooms. Maintain your faith, hope, and commitment to your profession. Life is cyclical. The good that you do will always come back!

Savory Morsel

A teacher affects eternity; he can never tell where his influence stops.

—Henry Adams (as cited in
Davidoff, 1952, p. 391)

Reflection Menu

- How do you see your profession as more than just a job to get a paycheck?
- In what ways do you create foundations that promote lifelong successes for your students?
- How will your academic feast be embellished now that you have read this text?

If You Like This Ingredient, You'll Also Like . . .

Ingredient 1

Ingredient 10

Bibliography

Bell, J. C. (1995). *Famous black quotations*. New York: Warner Books.

benShea, N. (2002). *Great quotes to inspire great teachers*. Thousand Oaks, CA: Corwin Press.

Carson, B. S. (1990). *Gifted hands*. Hagerstown, MD: Review and Herald.

Carson, B. S. (1992). *Think big: Unleashing your potential for excellence*. Grand Rapids, MI: Zondervan.

Corwin, M. (2000). *And still we rise*. New York: William Morrow.

Davidoff, H. (1952). *The pocket book of quotations*. New York: Pocket Books.

Jones, F. H. (2000). *Tools for teaching*. Santa Cruz, CA: Fred H. Jones & Associates.

Maxwell, J. C. (2003). *Attitude 101—What every leader needs to know*. Nashville, TN: Thomas Nelson.

McEwan, E. K. (2002). *10 traits of highly effective teachers*. Thousand Oaks, CA: Corwin Press.

Moran, C., Stobbe, J., Baron, W., Miller, J., & Moir, E. (2000). *Keys to the classroom: A teacher's guide to the first month of school* (2nd ed.). Thousand Oaks, CA: Corwin Press.

Schmoker, M. (2005). Here and now: Improving teaching and learning. In R. DuFour, R. Eaker, & R. DuFour (Eds.), *On common ground: The power of professional learning communities*. Bloomington, IN: National Educational Service.

Stock, G. (1987). *The book of questions*. New York: Workman.

Wilke, R. L. (2003). *The first days of class*. Thousand Oaks, CA: Corwin Press.

Wong, H., & Wong, R. (1998). *How to be an effective teacher: The first days of school*. Mountain View, CA: Harry K. Wong.

Recommended Reading

Arter, J., & McTighe, J. (2001). *Scoring rubrics in the classroom.* Thousand Oaks, CA: Corwin Press.

Barth, R. (1990). *Improving schools from within: Teachers, parents, and principals can make a difference.* San Francisco: Jossey-Bass.

Cattani, D. H. (2002). *A classroom of her own: How new teachers develop instructional, professional, and cultural competence.* Thousand Oaks, CA: Corwin Press.

Curwin, R. L. (2003). *Making good choices: Developing responsibility, respect, and self-discipline in Grades 4–9.* Thousand Oaks, CA: Corwin Press.

Delpit, L. (1995). *Other people's children: Cultural conflict in the classroom.* New York: New Press.

Glasgow, N. A., & Hicks, C. D. (2003). *What successful teachers do: 91 research-based classroom strategies for new and veteran teachers.* Thousand Oaks, CA: Corwin Press.

Hawley, W. D. (2002). *The keys to effective schools: Educational reform as continuous improvement.* Thousand Oaks, CA: Corwin Press.

House, S. N. (2002). *Behavior intervention manual: Goals, objectives, and intervention strategies.* Columbia, MO: Hawthorne Educational Services.

Jacobs, G. M., Power, M. A., & Wan, I. L. (2002). *The teacher's sourcebook for cooperative learning.* Thousand Oaks, CA: Corwin Press.

Jensen, E. (1998). *Teaching with the brain in mind.* Alexandria, VA: ASCD.

Johnson, R. (2002). *Using data to close the achievement gap.* Thousand Oaks, CA: Corwin Press.

Johnson, S. (1998). *Who moved my cheese?* New York: G.P. Putnam's Sons.

Jones, S. J. (2003). *Blueprint for student success: A guide to research-based teaching practices K–12.* Thousand Oaks, CA: Corwin Press.

Kottler, J. A., & Zehm, S. J. (2000). *On being a teacher: The human dimension.* Thousand Oaks, CA: Corwin Press.

Kuykendall, C. (1992). *From rage to hope.* Bloomington, IN: National Educational Service.

Marzano, R. (2001). *Classroom instruction that works: Research-based strategies for increasing student achievement.* Alexandria, VA: ASCD.

Stone, R. (2002). *Best practices for high school classrooms: What award-winning secondary teachers do.* Thousand Oaks, CA: Corwin Press.

Tomlinson, C. A. (2001). *How to differentiate instruction in mixed-ability classrooms.* Alexandria, VA: ASCD.

Villani, S. (2002). *Mentoring programs for new teachers: Models of induction and support.* Thousand Oaks, CA: Corwin Press.

Vitto, J. (2003). *Relationship-driven classroom management: Strategies that promote student motivation.* Thousand Oaks, CA: Corwin Press.

Wachter, J. C. (1999). *Sweating the small stuff: Answers to teachers' big problems.* Thousand Oaks, CA: Corwin Press.

Wiggins, G., & McTighe, J. (1998). *Understanding by design.* Alexandria, VA: ASCD.

Williamson, B. (1991). *101 ways to put pizzazz into your teaching.* Sacramento, CA: Dynamic Teaching Company.

Williamson, B. (1992). *Classroom management: A guidebook for success.* Sacramento, CA: Dynamic Teaching Company.

York-Barr, J., Sommers, W. A., Ghere, G. S., & Montie, J. (2001). *Reflective practice to improve schools: An action guide for educators.* Thousand Oaks, CA: Corwin Press.

Index